T0142558

erotic astrology

THE SEX SECRETS OF YOUR HOROSCOPE REVEALED

phyllis vega

Avon, Massachusetts

Published by
Adams Media, a division of F+W Media, Inc.
57 Littlefield Street
Avon, MA 02322
www.adamsmedia.com

ISBN-10: 1-60550-056-9
ISBN-13: 978-1-60550-056-0

Printed in the United States of America.

J I H G F E D C B A

Library of Congress Cataloging-in-Publication Data
is available from the publisher.

Contents

Dedication

To lovers and would-be lovers everywhere who are searching for some insight into what makes their partners tick

Introduction

You probably already know your Sun sign—the zodiacal sign that was occupied by the Sun on the day you were born. The Sun's placement in your natal chart is important, because it defines your basic character and personality, denotes your public persona, and determines how you act in social situations. However, for specific insight into the way you relate in more intimate situations, you need to look beyond the Sun to the sign position of the Moon, which deals with the inner self and shows how you come across emotionally. Even more important where your love life is concerned, are the horoscope placements of the celestial lovers, Mars (passion and sexuality) and Venus (love and romance).

Individuals are different, and act and react differently in amorous situations, based less on gender than on the positions of Mars and Venus in their horoscopes. Contrary to what you may have heard, both men *and* women are from Mars *and* Venus, because we all have both Mars and Venus in our birth charts. In astrology, the zodiacal positions of the Sun and Mars signify sexuality and physical expressions of desire, while the Moon and Venus symbolize love, romance, and emotional expressions of desire. The combination of your Sun sign with the sign Mars was in when you were born relates to your sex drive. Your Moon sign combined with the sign Venus was in at your birth denotes your love nature.

With *Erotic Astrology* in hand, you'll get to know yourself a lot better, find out what makes your lover tick, and learn whether or not you two are really compatible between the sheets. Moreover, you will be able to use the revelations of the stars to help you find true love and lasting passion, while avoiding many of the romantic pitfalls that make for disappointment in and out of the bedroom.

part 1

SUN AND MARS: YOUR SEX DRIVE

The Sun in your horoscope symbolizes the primary archetypal energy of your essential self. Its sign in your birth chart denotes your individuality and particularly personal approach to sexual experience. Mars, the embodiment of sexual energy, indicates your "sex quotient"—how you express (or repress) your sexuality, your attitude toward sex, the strength of your libido, your sexual prowess, and what turns you on or off.

The combination of the signs of the Sun and Mars in your birth chart reveals your sexual strengths and insecurities, and the role sexuality plays in your life. The sexual characteristics of each sign differ greatly, but by understanding the astrological dynamics of your own Sun/Mars combination, or that of your significant other or potential lover, you gain tremendous insight into one of the basic motivating forces of life: the sex drive.

1

Sun

THE SUN IS THE BRINGER OF LIGHT AND HEAT, without which our physical world would cease to exist. Therefore, it's not surprising that, in the ancient world, an all-seeing solar deity personified the Sun, and was viewed as an astute guarantor of justice. Today, in Western astrology, the Sun is regarded as the single most important factor in the natal horoscope chart. (If you're not sure of your Sun sign, you can look it up in the Sun Sign Chart in Appendix A.) The sign the Sun was in at the moment of your birth describes you as an individual, apart from any influences brought to bear by other people or the environment. The Sun's placement in your chart points out those life areas where you may be expected to shine. By indicating not only who you are, but also what you hope to become, your Sun sign reveals your future potential along with your current reality.

The Sun represents the masculine or yang principle. It relates to that part of you that is outer-directed and active in the material world. Positive attributes of the Sun include: creativity, self-confidence, warmth, courage, optimism, and magnanimity.

The Sun signs are divided into two main groups: the three Qualities (Cardinal, Fixed, and Mutable) that describe forms of expression, and the four Elements (Fire, Earth, Air, and Water) that describe temperament.

The Three Qualities

Individuals with the Sun in Cardinal signs (Aries, Cancer, Libra, and Capricorn) are the initiators and creators of the zodiac. Naturally ambitious and industrious, Cardinal natives willingly put a great deal of energy into achieving their objectives. Active individuals, they don't sit around waiting for things to come to them; they decide what they want and go after it. Born to be leaders, Cardinal types need to be the ones calling the shots.

Fixed sign Sun people (Taurus, Leo, Scorpio, and Aquarius) are steady, stable, and persistent. They have great reserves of power, but can be extremely stubborn and set in their ways. What they lack in bravery and bravado they make up for in resolve and determination; when they decide to do something they don't quit until their goal has been reached.

Those with the Sun in Mutable signs (Gemini, Virgo, Sagittarius, and Pisces) are flexible and resourceful. Like chameleons, they are adept at blending in with their surroundings. Their mental agility helps them deal successfully with a variety of situations. Because they see all sides of an issue and are easily influenced by outside forces, they often have great difficulty coming to firm decisions.

The Four Elements

People with the Sun in Fire signs (Aries, Leo, and Sagittarius) are self-motivated, aggressive, enthusiastic, and courageous. Fire sign individuals are the movers and shakers in society. Bursting with energy, they set a blistering pace. Whenever things quiet down they tend to get bored, and may leave in order to move on to something new and different.

Those with the Sun in Earth signs (Taurus, Virgo, and Capricorn) are prudent, stable, realistic, and pragmatic. Ever practical and concerned with security, Earth individuals are skilled in financial matters and good at using resources and managing people. Focused on the here and now, the Earth signs have a direct relationship with the physical world. Concepts and ideas hold less fascination for them than the knowledge and understanding gleaned from their own five senses.

Individuals with the Sun in Air signs (Gemini, Libra, and Aquarius) are highly skilled in the art of communication. Although innately intuitive, their basic nature is intellectual, rational, and analytical. They feel with their minds, and prefer to arrive at decisions through logic and careful reasoning. Since the air signs exist mainly in the realm of thoughts and ideas, they can be extremely distrustful of intense emotion.

People who have the Sun in Water signs (Cancer, Scorpio, and Pisces) are sensitive, intuitive, impressionable, and nurturing. They think with their emotions, and tend to follow their feelings no matter where they lead. Artistic by nature, watery types often have difficulty making rational decisions, and are at their best in situations that call for nonlinear reasoning or nonverbal communication. Their hunches are often correct and their natural psychic abilities help them to "know" things others don't.

Sign Compatibility

When considering sign compatibility, it is important to remember that, while some zodiacal combinations may be inherently easier or more difficult than others, no combination should ever be written off as impossible. In astrology, the general laws of sign compatibility hold true for all types of relationships. The rules are basically the same for lovers, married partners, parents and children, siblings, relatives, friends, professional associates, bosses and employees, coworkers, teachers and students, neighbors, and even casual acquaintances.

Traditionally, Fire signs get along best with Fire and Air; Air signs get along best with Air and Fire; Earth signs get along best with Earth and Water; Water signs get along best with Water and Earth. Conversely the blending of Fire with Earth, Fire with Water, Air with Earth, and Air with Water can be more difficult.

The Sun through the Signs of the Zodiac

The term zodiac refers to a circle of twelve constellations that lay on or near the ecliptic (the path the Sun travels in the course of a year). The sign it passes through modifies the Sun's energies and each of the twelve zodiacal signs brings out certain traits and inhibits others, without wholly changing the basic planetary energy.

Sun in Aries

With your Sun in fiery Aries your entire being is oriented toward action. You can put up with only so much inactivity, then you deliberately agitate things in an effort to get them moving again. Your perceptions are razor sharp, and you're inclined to follow your impulses and intuition. A quick learner and self-starter, you're curious, creative, and enthusiastic. Naturally competitive and perpetually testing the limits of your abilities, you welcome all types of challenges, but long for instant gratification. As a result, you don't always hang around to see your projects through to a conclusion. Your driving need to always be first makes you assertive, aggressive, and an enterprising natural leader. Given a cause to fight for, your typical response is to suit up for battle. Never one to look before you leap, you jump right in to defend those who can't defend themselves.

In Bed

The typical ram is energetic and aggressive, adores the challenge, chase, and conquest of new romance, and exudes sex appeal. Your approach to life and sexuality tends to be all or nothing, and you don't like being teased, put off, or kept waiting. Naturally impatient and impulsive, you know what you want, and you want it now. Since you take great pride in your prowess between the sheets, once you feel you've been given the go ahead, there's no turning back

Sexually you're a fireball and, when aroused, you can be more ardent and exciting than any sign in the zodiac, except possibly Scorpio. Your ego, however, is rather fragile and the best way to woo you is with a little flattery. Although you're usually open to straight talk, the lover who is foolish enough to critique your performance in bed needs to choose his or her words very carefully. Where criticism is concerned, you are a lot more comfortable dishing it out than taking it. To you, even a slight hint that your lovemaking is less than perfect can be devastating.

More a tiger than a ram where your sexuality is concerned, you're turned on by the hunt as well as the conquest. A decidedly physical and fearless lover, you've been blessed with the stamina to keep going all night long. In your quest for sexual pleasure, you enjoy variety, experimentation, and innovation. An open-minded bed partner is virtually a must for you, because boredom is anathema. Although eroticism matters, a mental connection with your bedmate is also truly important. In love, as in life, you definitely want it all.

Turn-ons & Turn-offs

Nothing turns you on faster than a partner who takes you by surprise in the bedroom. Although ultraromantic when it suits your mood, you nevertheless enjoy a bawdy romp in the hay. Your idea of a turn-on is a passionate, exhilarating lover who challenges you mentally as well as physically. While emotional games are a no-no in the ram's world, you adore intellectual and physical ones. In a game of Truth or Dare, you're not afraid to own up to the truth, yet you can't resist a dare.

True to Aries' desire to be first in everything, you enjoy making love early in the morning. You have no compunctions when it comes to trying new things; the more outrageous and exciting the innovations, the more you like them. You're fond of little presents, especially sex toys specifically designed to increase excitement and pleasure. The head is your most powerful erogenous zone, so stroking your hair and rubbing your scalp relaxes you and heightens your sensations. You thrive on impulse and surprise, and the advances of a bold, inventive lover who catches you unaware provides a guaranteed turn-on.

You're a doer, not a dreamer. Your fantasies, if you have any, all take place inside your head and don't seem like fantasies to you. Your tendency to dramatize your life and envision yourself as a mythological hero is not playacting, it's an integral part of who you are. Sexy role-playing games hold little appeal for you, because the only larger-than-life character you care to play is *you*. For an Aries, sex for its own sake, without any personal connection, is a definite turn-off. You like sex, and want it to be spicy, exciting, and fun. Yet, even in the absence of grand passion and lifelong devotion, you expect genuine warmth and a feeling of camaraderie between you and your bedmate.

Sexual Synergy

Aries with Aries: While this matchup is rarely boring, neither is it tranquil. Your nights are filled with passion and romance and your days with true companionship. Yet your sense of togetherness is often threatened by the fiery chemistry of your competitive natures. Fights are inevitable, but you both forgive easily—and the making up is awesome.

Aries with Taurus: Despite the differences in temperament, you complement each other in ways that count. The tranquil bull adds stability and serenity to the ram's madcap life. In bed, the bold ram guides the shy bull to new heights of sexual pleasure. If problems arise it's often because Aries demands freedom, and Taurus tends to be rather possessive.

Aries with Gemini: Since both are active and have an unquenchable desire for new experiences, you're rarely bored. Some differences may develop because Aries is intensely passionate, and Gemini doesn't take love or sex all that seriously. However, you're both curious and open to engaging in sexual experimentation.

Aries with Cancer: Although Fire and Water don't mix well, a strong physical attraction and psychic bond can develop between the ram and the crab. You are both ardent, sensuous, and romantic, and sexually you two can be very compatible. However, if insecure Cancer gets overly emotional, insensitive Aries may lose patience and take off.

Aries with Leo: As a couple, you two are temperamentally and sexually well suited. Leo is loyal and affectionate, and Aries is dynamic and exciting. You're both self-motivated, and concerned with your own work and interests. Whereas Aries likes to win, Leo needs to rule. This matchup works best when the ram lets the lion play the role of boss.

Aries with Virgo: The ram is temperamental and outspoken, and the reserved virgin is totally unequipped to handle emotional scenes. Virgo is critical, which Aries can't stand, and Virgo's penchant for analysis drives Aries crazy. Still, there is passion smoldering beneath Virgo's cool facade, and hot, sexy Aries knows how to release it.

Aries with Libra: The chemistry between you two is strong, and love-making will be pleasurable and mutually rewarding. Moreover, you're both fun-loving and gregarious, and enjoy an active social life. Even so, the ram can be driven to distraction by the scales' indecisiveness, and Libra may feel pressured by Aries' super-fast decision making.

Aries with Scorpio: Sexually, these two signs are well matched, because both partners are passionate, energetic, highly sexual, and adventurous. However, the ram tends to view the act of love as exciting, pleasurable, and fun, whereas the intense scorpion is almost always seeking a deeper connection that is spiritually and emotionally transforming.

Aries with Sagittarius: Each of these fiery individualists is idealistic and affectionate, with a life affirming, healthy attitude toward love, sex, and intimacy. Physically and mentally, you two are well matched. However, Aries tends to be more demanding and emotional, and may look upon tolerant Sagittarius as detached and impersonal.

Aries with Capricorn: As romantic partners, impulsive Aries and cautious Capricorn have some formidable obstacles to overcome. Socially, goats tend to be rather reserved, whereas rams are outgoing and vivacious. While seemingly prudish, Capricorn actually has one of the stronger libidos in the zodiac, and is turned-on by Aries' sex appeal.

Aries with Aquarius: Each of you brings additional excitement and unpredictability into the other's life. Fiery, demonstrative Aries may secretly wish the Aquarius lover were more passionate. However, any lack of ardor is more than compensated for by the water bearer's love of experimentation and willingness to try new things—in the bedroom and out.

Aries with Pisces: Temperamentally you are quite different, but your differences are complementary. Ethereal Pisces appeals to the romantic side of Aries' nature, and the ram may be seduced by the fish's need for protection. Aries gets off on Pisces' erotic fantasies and instinctive sexuality, but the ram's boldness can overwhelm the timid fish.

Sun in Taurus

Sensible and concerned with the practical necessities of life, Taurus is generally considered the earthiest of the three Earth signs. Your tranquil, easygoing nature inclines toward beauty and harmony in all things. Introverted, you prefer to sit back and wait for opportunity to come knocking. Unswerving in your devotion to physical reality and the security of the tangible world, you're not attracted to the realm of nebulous ideas. Your friends and relations count on you for material help and support, because you take your commitments seriously. Home and family come first with you, and you're not likely to run off at the first sign of trouble.

As a member of one of the most reliable zodiac signs, you carefully guard your image of respectability. Despite your innate good nature and amiable sense of humor, you dislike being made to look foolish. Although not actually lazy, the bull patently refuses to waste energy. Better at finishing projects than starting them, you think and plan, but have an awful time taking the first step. Although you cannot be rushed, when left to your own devices you do a great job.

On an emotional level, however, bulls can be totally clueless. Remarkably ignorant of your own inner makeup, you have limited understanding of what makes people tick, and virtually no interest in finding out. Naturally reticent, you rarely share your inner thoughts with anyone, and sometimes your loved ones may feel shut out.

In Bed

Sexually, those born under the sign of the bull are deeply passionate, although somewhat reserved. Fearful of rejection, you prefer to draw love to you rather than pursue it openly. Since Taurus is naturally charming, alluring, and sexy, you probably have little trouble attracting romantic partners. When intimately involved with someone, you make a caring, considerate lover. However, you require a lot of affection and consideration in return, and thrive on flattery and compliments.

To you, good sex usually means a sensuous, passionate, and uncomplicated physical relationship. Your ideas about love tend to be traditional. You refuse to play games, and you don't make promises that you can't keep. You are naturally seductive, and when you overcome your inhibitions you're capable of depths of passion that will leave your lover gasping for breath—and begging for more. Once your libido has been let loose, you're a very demanding lover. However, you're set in your ways and not generally given to kinky boudoir behavior or radical sexual experimentation.

In your love life, as in all other things, you cannot be rushed. Your sensuality, generosity, affectionate nature, and legendary staying power make you an excellent lover and sex is closely tied to your love of pleasure and luxury. You absolutely adore everything that is sensual and romantic from satin sheets, flowers, perfume, and music, to champagne, chocolates, exotic fruits, and other delicious edible treats. Your bedmate is practically guaranteed a sexual experience that is joyful, pleasurable, and extremely satisfying.

Turn-ons & Turn-offs

Taurus is arguably the most sensuous sign in the zodiac. You thoroughly enjoy the one-on-one aspect of a romantic relationship, and the affection and intimacy it provides. In private, you make an intense bedmate; one who is happy to have the sensual encounters continue all night long. Sexually, Taurus is the Energizer Bunny of the zodiac. You thrive on unhurried nights of love play, liberally punctuated with amorous conversation, erotic fantasy, and an occasional indulgence in food and drink.

The bull craves a partner who is loving, yet strong and practical. The suitor who arrives bearing gifts and kind words easily wins your heart, since Taurus is responsive to both material goods and heartfelt compliments. Making you feel safe and secure is a smart strategy for any potential lover. What you want most is to live in a comfortable world and have a special someone to share it with.

One-night stands are not your style. You regard lovemaking as an art; and when you go to bed with someone, it's to make love, not to have sex. Elegant surroundings, sensuous perfumes, silky fabrics, soft music, and sex-play involving delectable delicacies such as whipped cream or chocolate are guaranteed turn-ons. You particularly enjoy being kissed around the neck and throat, and having your skin gently stroked sets your whole body on fire. For you, making love is a process that inevitably involves wooing and protracted foreplay. Luxury loving and pleasure-oriented, you take your time in bed. Your ideal lover moves in slowly, savoring every moment, and builds gradually to a powerful climax.

Sexual Synergy

Taurus with Aries: You two tend to approach life quite differently. Yet, despite your differences, passionate, romantic Aries poses an irresistible challenge to sensuous, affectionate, romantic Taurus. Even when your ideas are poles apart, life is a lot more interesting when slow-moving Taurus and fiery Aries form an intimate alliance.

Taurus with Taurus: This may not be the most exciting romantic combination, but it's rock solid. Each of you is steady, reliable, practical, and devoted to home and family. A close relationship between you is virtually guaranteed to be emotionally comforting and sexually satisfying. Boredom poses the only threat to a happy, long-lasting union.

Taurus with Gemini: Sexually and emotionally both partners find a romantic union stimulating, exciting, and satisfying. However, the bull is likely to grow weary of hearing Gemini chatter on and on, and the swift-moving twin could become increasingly annoyed by Taurus's slow reactions and stubborn, plodding nature.

Taurus with Cancer: Sexually and romantically this is a near perfect match. Both are homebodies and appreciate the simple joys of a comfortable domestic life. Even so, difficulties may arise because Taurus is stubborn and intractable, Cancer is moody and thin-skinned, and neither of you is inclined to talk about what's really bothering you.

Taurus with Leo: Be prepared for a battle of wills between the irresistible force (Leo) and the immovable object (Taurus). Still, this can be a surprisingly loving and successful romantic union. Each of you is affectionate and loyal, and you share a desire for luxury and the many other goodies life has to offer.

Taurus with Virgo: This pair is nicely matched sexually and love-making is erotic and intense. Virgo may be slower to arouse, but Taurus's patience is legendary. With tenderness and affection, the bull easily melts the virgin's reserve. This twosome works well as long as Virgo avoids criticism, and Taurus keeps overindulgences to a minimum.

Taurus with Libra: Both love peace and harmony, and strive to avoid conflict and tension as much as possible. The affable sweetness in each of your natures makes for a pleasant relationship. While the bull's stability and persistence anchors the scales' airy indecisiveness, Libra's easygoing approach to life can drive Taurus up a wall.

Taurus with Scorpio: The magnetic attraction you feel for each other can overcome any lack of common interests, and a physical relationship between you could be intense and long lasting. Even so, straightforward Taurus may be put off by the sly scorpion's deviousness, and thin-skinned Scorpio can misinterpret the bull's playful sense of humor.

Taurus with Sagittarius: Despite their lack of commonality, Taurus is drawn to outgoing, exciting, fun-loving Sagittarius. The passionate bull may enjoy the archer's lusty sexuality, but is easily irked by Sagittarius' devil-may-care attitude toward love. Taurus is settled and longs for security, and Sagittarius is a gambler and wanderer.

Taurus with Capricorn: This pairing of Earth signs usually results in a good match. Both of you want the emotional and material security of a stable, long-lasting relationship. Each of you has strong sexual needs and desires, however the goat's passion often burns well beneath the surface and the bull may have to bring it out.

Taurus with Aquarius: The only traits you two have in common are stubbornness and a reluctance to change your ways. Even so, Taurus may be intrigued by the freewheeling water bearer's openness to sexual experimentation and willingness to explore new erotic techniques, and Fixed Aquarius is likely to appreciate the bull's loyalty and dependability.

Taurus with Pisces: In bed, sensual, romantic Taurus can easily get caught up in Pisces' dreamy, erotic fantasies. The lovemaking between you two is likely to be sensuous and satisfying. But ultimately, the pragmatic, straightforward bull could be irritated by the enigmatic, impractical fish's inability to deal with day-to-day realities.

Sun in Gemini

Physically and mentally alert, the Gemini twins are among the fastest moving members of the zodiacal family. Best known for your ability to communicate, you love to talk. Geminis are intellectually inclined, forever probing people and places in search of new information. Although interested in virtually everything, you're not predisposed to delve too deeply into any one subject. There is just too much to do, see, talk about, and learn, for you to plumb the depths of a single topic or stick with any one thing for very long.

Like the twins that symbolize your Sun sign, you have two distinct sides to your character. In all likelihood, one twin is a happy-go-lucky, extroverted social butterfly, while the other is moody, erratic, and introspective. Although you can be indecisive and wishy-washy, changing your mind or mood on a whim, this flexibility allows you to go with the flow. Naturally adaptable and dexterous, you're capable of tackling many different projects at once. The downside of such an inquisitive, probing mind, however, can be a lack of staying power.

In Bed

Although easygoing and relaxed about sexuality, in the bedroom airy Gemini can be as bold and daring as any fiery Aires. However, while you thoroughly enjoy the physical act of lovemaking, and love being in love, sex is rarely the main thing on your mind. The *idea* of lovemaking often attracts a Gemini more than the act itself.

Once you set your sights on a perspective lover, you know all the right things to do and say to gain his or her attention. With the mood upon you, you're capable of making love just about anywhere and glib enough to talk your way into virtually any bed. Flirting comes easy to you, and when the sexual banter becomes hot and heavy you may surprise a fairly recent acquaintance with an impromptu invitation to join you in a passionate night of lovemaking. However, if the new relationship progresses to the nitty-gritty of serious commitment, you're just as likely to hit the panic button.

Although the Gemini lover is often in too much of a hurry to bother with courting rituals, when you do take the time to sweet talk your partner, you say whatever you think he or she wants to hear. Moreover, you're totally sincere in what you say—even if only for the moment. One minute you can be totally solicitous and responsive to your lover's needs and feelings, and the next you are off on some new tangent and apparently cannot care less.

Turn-ons & Turn-offs

There is no doubt that your major erogenous zone is located inside your head. Nothing turns you on faster, or more completely, than wit and charm, and you are aroused by erotic words and clever, evocative quips. Phone sex must have been invented by a Gemini. The same goes for the hot and heavy sexual banter that takes place in online chat rooms and via e-mail. Although you respond amorously to tactile pleasures, it's sharing your erotic thoughts and dreams with your lover that really gets you going. Lusty words (yours or your partner's) engage your vivid imagination—and inflame your libido.

The Gemini nature is so changeable, that it is difficult to say exactly what you will like from one sexual encounter to the next. The twins' aversion to boredom is legendary. You consider variety the most important ingredient in lovemaking and thrive on innovation and versatility. You equate sex with fun, and enjoy engaging in fantasy and role-playing games. Moreover, Geminis are fantastic kissers, and enjoy doing it. Restless and perpetually on the go, the typical Gemini has a somewhat nervous temperament. Sex play relaxes you, and soaking in a tub or spa with your partner prior to lovemaking helps sooth your jangled nerves.

Since you were born under the most unpredictable sign in the zodiac, the only thing your lover can truly count on is that anything is possible. An adventurous lover, you long to please and be pleased. If you don't know what your partner likes, you ask.

Sexual Synergy

Gemini with Aries: This lively, energetic pairing makes for good friends as well as good lovers. Both of you thrive on constant activity and variety. Moreover, you enjoy each other's humor and share a preference for an active social life. There will be bedroom high jinks, because you're both enthusiastic about sex.

Gemini with Taurus: You're intrigued by the bull's uncomplicated directness, and Taurus responds to the twin's devil-may-care attitude.

There is rarely a dull moment when fast-talking Gemini leads Taurus on a merry chase. But the bull wants life to be stable and ordered, and you're easily bored and always searching for new experiences.

Gemini with Gemini: The pace is frenetic, and you two are never bored when you're together. Sharing dreams and ideas makes you feel like true soul mates. Sex for Gemini is fun and games, so you're both open to trying anything new and different. But emotional coolness and the need to overanalyze everything may open up a huge gulf between you.

Gemini with Cancer: Temperamentally, the two of you are not at all alike. Cancer is sensitive and emotional, and Gemini's a cool intellectual. Moreover, the crab's mood swings are about as frequent as the twins' mind changes. Even so, adoring Cancer is able to fulfill all your sexual fantasies, and your cheerfulness can brighten up a crabby disposition.

Gemini with Leo: This is a lively, fun-loving combination that works great as long as you're willing to concede center stage to the lion or lioness. Each is super sociable and enjoys a good party, but Leo demands loyalty and won't tolerate Gemini's flirtatious ways. Both of you are playful, passionate, amorous lovers, and in bed you set off sparks.

Gemini with Virgo: Both of these signs love to talk, but neither of you is comfortable opening up and expressing your true feelings. Sexually, you're on different wavelengths, yet romantic Virgo can be swept away by Gemini's fast-talking seductive manner. Despite the differences in temperament, you two share many common interests in and out of the bedroom.

Gemini with Libra: Librans can't make up their minds, and Geminis are always changing theirs. Still, you make an affectionate, fun-loving couple that enjoys an active social life, and adores entertaining and travel. Each of you is fervent in bed, yet neither is jealous or demanding. Libra usually goes along with Gemini's taste for sexual diversity.

Gemini with Scorpio: Gemini's airy openness is hard for serious, secretive Scorpio to comprehend, and the scorpion's burning intensity frightens and fascinates the twins. Nevertheless, your differences can serve as the spark that ignites your sexual passion. However, even with strong physical attraction, an ongoing relationship may be difficult.

Gemini with Sagittarius: These two zodiacal opposites attract each other like magnets. Because of your wide-ranging and varied interests, you complement each other. Each of you has a fun-and-games attitude toward love and romance. In the bedroom, anything goes with this combination, which usually translates into exhilarating sexual encounters.

Gemini with Capricorn: This is one of the more difficult combinations. The dependable, serious goat considers Gemini irresponsible and unpredictable. Although Capricorn finds the twins' lack of reserve embarrassing, deep down the lusty goat admires Gemini's freewheeling sexual attitude, and may secretly yearn for the audacity to emulate it.

Gemini with Aquarius: Your compatibility is virtually assured. You take great pleasure in each other's company, and any sexual union between you can be truly exciting. Each of you view love as an extremely enjoyable part of life, but friendship and true companionship mean more to both of you.

Gemini with Pisces: The passion quotient is likely to be high in this match-up, but so are the inevitable problems. Gemini needs freedom and new vistas; Pisces craves unending adoration. The fish doesn't feel secure with the gadabout twins, and attempts to pull the net tighter. Still, Pisces is enigmatic and mysterious, and Gemini loves solving mysteries.

Sun in Cancer

Although moody is the word most often used to describe Cancer, crabs come in all types from the shy and withdrawn to some of the most sociable, outgoing, well-known members of society. Your inner nature is sympathetic, with a psychic-like sensitivity to the moods and feelings of those around you. Cancers are typically nurturing, empathetic, and appreciative of the nest-like quality of a secure home base. Having people to care for helps you feel useful, and provides you with a sense of security and belonging.

Secretive and self-protective, you prefer working beneath the surface of any situation, rather than confronting it head-on. You instinctively know the best way to manipulate circumstances and people and, like the crab, which moves sideways, you'll do everything possible to avoid an out-and-out showdown. Normally gentle, kind, and caring, you lash out when your feelings are hurt. When angry or upset, the crab transforms into a sharp-tongued, vindictive, vengeful harpy. Cancer has one of the longest memories in the zodiac, and never gets over a slight. You may forgive, but you don't forget!

In Bed

The Cancer lover makes a wonderfully imaginative sweetheart who loves to kiss and cuddle. Both shy and sensual, you can be passionate on the one hand, and affectionate and tender on the other. Moreover, you are enough of a sexual athlete to please your partner fully. All it takes is a little encouragement to help you overcome your fear of rejection.

In love and romance, as in everything else in life, you cannot be rushed or coerced. Crabs are old fashioned in and out of the bedroom, and both males and females want to be wooed before they are won. You want to be cared for and cherished, and you like caring for and cherishing your beloved in return. In bed, you're as concerned with pleasing your partner as you are about your own pleasure. The typical crab is intuitive; you can generally sense what your lover wants, which makes your encounter between the sheets a finely tuned physical and emotional union.

The firepower that can be aroused in you is more likely to manifest as a series of fantasies and less as an exercise in sexual acrobatics. You enjoy making love and being made love to. The lover who engages your mind and imagination with humor and lively conversation also enlivens your spirits. In the crab's world, sex and lust often equal love and its nurturing aspects (such as home and hearth). Crabs aren't overly comfortable with sexual experimentation and any show of vulgarity from a lover can be off putting, especially early on. The caring partner who is able to appeal to and satisfy your deep-seated need for security is likely to unleash a volcanic eruption of sensual delights.

Turn-ons & Turn-offs

The crab's favorite fantasy generally includes good food and great sex. Any artful combination of these two sensual activities is virtually guaranteed to turn you on. Preparing and eating a luscious feast together with your lover evokes an atmosphere of voluptuous indulgence. A private encounter that begins in the kitchen, and ends with you feeding each other delectable little snacks in bed, can turn into an erotic free-for-all.

The breast and chest are erogenous zones for most people, but this is especially true for those born under the sign of the crab. You enjoy having your chest stroked, and respond passionately to oral and manual manipulation of the nipples. Cancer's fascination for moonlight and water makes a seaside outing, where you can hear the pounding of the ocean as you make love, the perfect choice for an erotic getaway. If a trip to the ocean is not feasible, playing a nature sounds machine in your bedroom can evoke many of the same feelings. The right atmosphere, replete with scented candles and aromatic massage oils usually does the trick. Deep down you long to be seduced and swept away on a wave of passion. Once awakened, your lusty libido will carry you and your partner to the heights of ecstatic pleasure.

Cancer is a deeply private sign, and you need to feel safe before you reveal yourself. Nothing turns you off faster than a prospective partner who comes on too strong, or tries to push you into intimacy before you're ready. You're too sensitive and romantic to respond to a blunt sexual appeal. Even in a long-term union, you prefer the indirect approach, and rarely come right out and say you want sex. For you, a sense of physical and emotional well-being is a must. Without a partner who understands this, you're likely to log a great deal of time inside your pesky crab shell.

Sexual Synergy

Cancer with Aries: Both are passionate, sensuous, romantic, and sentimental, and sexually you two can be very compatible. However, problems may develop when upbeat Aries gets a taste of the crab's sullen moods. The ram's need for autonomy and independence frequently conflicts with Cancer's desire for closeness, intimacy, and mutual dependency.

Cancer with Taurus: This combination often results in a near perfect match-up in both the kitchen and the bedroom. Together you make passionate, affectionate domestic partners who are usually on the same sexual wavelength. The main obstacles to total contentment are the bull's legendary stubbornness and the crab's frequent mood swings.

Cancer with Gemini: Gemini views the world through a mental window, while Cancer sees it through a cloud of emotion. Curious Gemini enjoys experimentation, while the crab, though passionate, is sexually conservative and emotionally possessive. Still, the freewheeling twins can help the uptight crab emerge from its shell and have more fun.

Cancer with Cancer: While not the most exciting pairing in the zodiac, this coupling can be one of the longest lasting, especially since neither likes letting go. Serious differences may arise because both are sensitive, moody, and easily hurt. Even so, you understand each other so completely that this can be a very rewarding union of genuine soul mates.

Cancer with Leo: Sexually, these two are almost always compatible, especially if the lion is willing to demonstrate enough love, consideration, and devotion to reassure the insecure crab. Leo's sunny self-confidence acts as a stabilizer for Cancer's moody insecurity, and the crab's readiness to offer praise fulfills the lion's need for adoration.

Cancer with Virgo: Cancer is much more emotional than the shy, reserved virgin. Virgos, however, are incurable romantics, and crabs are absolute suckers for romance. Each is inclined to mood changes that, at times, can irritate the other. Still, this is a good match so long as the super critical virgin avoids hurting sensitive Cancer's tender feelings.

Cancer with Libra: Your basic temperaments are very different. Although airy Libra is the sign of partnership, the scales are more emotionally detached than the clinging crab, and dislike being tied down. Major problems can arise if Cancer becomes excessively possessive. The more the crab tries to hold on, the harder Libra struggles to break free.

Cancer with Scorpio: This is generally an excellent match. When the passionate, emotional crab and the highly sexed scorpion get together, sparks fly. The hyper-intense emotionality of your relationship fosters a deep, lasting bond. There may be some melodramatic rows between you, but the making-up afterward will be heavenly.

Cancer with Sagittarius: Sagittarius longs for freedom and adventure, whereas Cancer is home and family-oriented. Given your opposite goals, you two make an odd couple. Even so, your dissimilarities complement each other. The crab finds the archer exciting, and Sagittarius gets Cancer to abandon the shell and live a little.

Cancer with Capricorn: These two opposite signs have a lot in common. You share similar goals: success, security, and a stable home life. The crab and the goat are both highly sexed, and your physical union should be imbued with passion. But Cancer is warm and caring, and Capricorn can come off as cool and emotionally detached.

Cancer with Aquarius: Although Aquarian independence may intrigue Cancer, these two signs have little in common. The crab responds emotionally; the water bearer is mainly influenced by ideas. While this isn't an easy match, you two should get along fine in the bedroom. With a little effort to understand each other you can overcome your differences.

Cancer with Pisces: These Water signs have a natural affinity, both sexually and emotionally. Both are ardent, affectionate lovers with an inclination toward romance and a desire to make the honeymoon last forever. Since both are extremely sensitive, each should be extra careful to avoid hurting the other's feelings.

Sun in Leo

Leo, like the Sun, shines with stellar incandescence. Never one to shy away from the limelight, you can be found wherever the action is the thickest. Courageous, enthusiastic, and ambitious, you love dramatizing your experiences, and thrive on excitement and adulation. The typical lion is "on" most of the time, and fame and recognition are infinitely more important to you than either money or power. Even the most timid pussycat is an actor at heart. Moreover, the role you assume is a noble one, and you abhor anything mean or petty.

The regal lion feels entitled to the best life has to offer. You willingly share what you have with others, especially your loved ones. A take-charge person, your self-assurance and optimism inspire confidence in those around you. Although the lion is often accused of being bossy, what you really want is to be *the* boss. You like to make your own decisions and strongly resent being told what to do. When you achieve your heart's desire—recognition as leader—you usually refrain from bossing others around. However, you actually enjoy helping other people manage their lives, and if you're not careful you could end up trying to run them.

The infamous Leo pride is no myth. Anyone who wants to get along with you will refrain from stepping on your toes or wounding your ego. Loyalty is your maxim. You repay those who stick by you and give you what you consider your due, by doing whatever it takes to justify their confidence in you. However, those who disappoint you, hurt your pride, or let you down will hear the lion roar.

In Bed

As befits their fiery Sun sign, lions possess a robust, consistent sex drive. You throw yourself wholeheartedly into eroticism, and make an ardent, passionate, inventive bedmate. However, Leo's Fixed element makes you considerably less aggressive in initiating sexual contact than the other two Fire signs (Aries and Sagittarius.) You prefer relying on your devastating charm and magnetic sex appeal to draw potential lovers to you.

As a member of a Fixed sign, you dislike change. Despite your passionate nature, there is a touch of conservatism in your pleasure seeking that prevents you from straying too far outside traditional boundaries. Ever attentive to your partner's needs and desires, you expect your consideration to be reciprocated. Although your sexual prowess may be up there with the most ardent Aries or Scorpio, your leonine ego requires frequent encouragement and reassurance. The mate who hopes to win and keep your heart should remember that lions need to feel cherished and admired, as well as loved.

Turn-ons & Turn-offs

Leo is the most ardent and attentive of bedmates, but you would rather be alone than involved with the wrong person. The royal lion is status conscious, and something of a snob. You must be able to respect and admire the person you love, and your ideal partner is intelligent, dignified, and classy. More than anything, your lover must always remember who is number one, and act on this knowledge at all times.

You're a star in the bedroom, you know it, and want to be certain that your partner knows it too. The lion loves seduction and foreplay. For you, making love is an art form, and fulfilling your erotic fantasies is a major turn-on.

Sensual, unhurried lovemaking in lavish comfort appeals to you more than grabbing a quickie before rushing off to the office. The back is Leo's most sensitive area, and sweeping caresses over your back and spine sexually stimulate and excite you. You enjoy building anticipation for an erotic encounter by setting up the scene in advance. Sexy attire turns you on, as does dressing or undressing your partner. Although you usually prefer wooing or being wooed luxuriously (as befits your regal status), the freewheeling, spontaneous part of your love-nature is rejuvenated by unplanned moments. An occasional bit of impromptu, devil-may-care lovemaking can inflame your desires and keep your sex life fresh and new.

Sexual Synergy

Leo with Aries: There is a lot of energy and excitement in this pairing. Sexually, the sparks will fly. Temperamentally it's a good match, because each of you is idealistic, optimistic, and outgoing. Despite the harmony, volatile, hot-tempered individuals are sure to clash. When you do, your battles will be boisterous and dramatic.

Leo with Taurus: The combination of these two strong-willed, Fixed-sign individuals can be challenging, to say the least. Everything should go very well, especially in the bedroom, until you two fail to see eye-to-eye on something. Compromise is necessary to make this pairing successful.

Leo with Gemini: This mixture of Fire and Air can be great as long as the twins don't try to manipulate the lion or steal the regal star's audience. Leo is jealous, and may begin to resent Gemini's independent, freewheeling lifestyle. Still, you two have fun together, in the bedroom and out, and you're not likely to grow bored or tire of each other's company.

Leo with Cancer: This pairing can be difficult because of your different temperaments, but it is definitely doable. Leo is flattered by Cancer's worshipful attention, yet resentful of the crab's emotional neediness. Even so, you two have a lot in common. You both want to live in the grand manner that comes with success, affluence, and social prestige.

Leo with Leo: Romantically you two get along famously, with lots of hot sex and fun at the outset. However, both need to be the center of attention, and neither wants to share the starring role with the other. If your union turns into a competition, the relationship may fizzle out.

Leo with Virgo: This isn't the easiest combination in the zodiac. Leo is sensitive to criticism and likely to regard Virgo's idea of "constructive criticism" as a personal attack. In bed, however, the exciting lion inflames the imagination of the hesitant virgin. Because of Virgo's flexibility, this match can work as long as Leo has the starring role.

Leo with Libra: This blend of Fire and Air sounds ideal, but there are possible pitfalls. Both of you are romantics, and your sex life should be hot. However, Leo normally sees life in terms of "I" not "we," whereas Libra, born under the sign of partnership, tends to think in pairs.

Leo with Scorpio: The question here is not whether you two get along in the bedroom; it's if you can stand each other in the rest of the house. Both of you tend to be dictatorial and domineering. Scorpio's dark secrecy presents a sharp contrast to Leo's sunny optimism. This all-or-nothing union only works if both pull in the same direction.

Leo with Sagittarius: The sexual relationship between you two is sure to be fiery and exciting. However, the archer refuses to take love seriously, and this tendency to avoid commitment could bother the more settled lion. Short term you'll surely have a wonderful time together, but may have to work at sustaining a life-long union.

Leo with Capricorn: The goat's emotionally detached, reserved attitude presents a sharp contrast to the lion's warm enthusiasm and cheerful temperament. Nevertheless, there is a solid sexual energy between you, and you may enjoy many passionate bedroom romps. You both honor your commitments, and prize loyalty and fidelity above all else.

Leo with Aquarius: Opposites attract, and Leo is often intrigued by the water bearer's oddball originality. But the more conventional lion may be turned off by Aquarius's anything goes approach to lovemaking. Although you're both upfront and sincere, your Fixed natures make you extremely stubborn and sometimes intractable.

Leo with Pisces: You two function on totally different psychological levels. The fish dwells on an emotional inner plane, whereas the lion is extroverted and action-oriented. Nevertheless, mysterious, mystical Pisces fascinates the worldly lion. Easily enchanted by Pisces' flattery and adulation, when the fish seeks protection, the lion eagerly obliges.

Sun in Virgo

Virgos are high-strung bundles of nervous energy and, with your mind operating in overdrive, it's exceedingly difficult for you to kick back and relax. Precise in your labors and literal in your approach, you pay a great deal of attention to detail. Your inclination is to delve deeper and be more critical than everyone else. Your propensity for overanalyzing and agonizing over every little thing causes you a lot of unnecessary mental stress and strain. Compelled to explore all possible options, you often have great difficulty making concrete decisions.

Your sweet, caring nature and natural wit and charm allow you make friends quite easily. You are, however, cautious about people and slow to commit to new relationships. The friends you do have are important to you, and you tend to hold onto them for a really long time. You may have some pals who are much younger or much older than you. Age differences don't bother you, because you choose your friends based on shared interests. If you can't be with people who stimulate you mentally, you'd rather be out on your own or at home with your family or pets.

In Bed

Misinterpretation of the connection between the Sun sign Virgo, and the dictionary definition of the word *virginity*, can lead to the false assumption that everyone born under this sign must be chaste. However, in ancient times the word "virgin" actually signified purity of intent rather than chastity. Although your surface demeanor is reserved and undemonstrative, deep down you are warm and caring; and with the right partner you're as sexy and sensual as any member of the zodiacal family.

Virgos have discriminating tastes. When making love, you strive for a memorable experience that is pleasing to both partners, and you expect the same consideration that you show your bedmate. You enjoy touching and being touched, and your heightened sensory perception enhances your physical pleasure. You particularly enjoy foreplay that begins with kisses and languid caresses. Never one to rush, you take the time to slowly build to a prolonged state of ecstasy. It doesn't take a lot of exotic thrills to entice you, but you do appreciate the beauty and comfort of clean, elegantly appointed surroundings. A romantic ambiance with soft lighting, music, fresh flowers, and scented candles puts you in the mood for an evening of loving.

Turn-ons & Turn-offs

You appreciate a bed partner who occasionally takes the lead and comes up with ways of making your sex life more exciting. The stomach area is very sensitive for Virgo; circular motion and gentle massages with the fingertips or tongue on your stomach area and around your belly button are guaranteed turn-ons. A provocative striptease also intrigues you, and can add a mood of delightful decadence to your lovemaking. Although the idea of trying new things such as sex toys may shock you at first, under the right circumstances they add a playful, slightly naughty aspect to your bedroom activities. With encouragement, your own hidden desires morph into a tempestuous passion.

Inwardly, you may be shy and reserved, but a patient, thoughtful lover who draws out your controlled desires will be well rewarded. While bedroom drama doesn't appeal to you, sexy role-playing fantasy games can be a major turn-on. You like variety and enjoy experimenting with different positions and techniques. After a grueling workday, an erotic massage with warm, naturally scented oils relaxes you and soothes your jangled nerves. Although you may need a little coaxing, your dormant passions ignite as you unwind.

A true romantic, you enjoy courtship. You're turned on by poetry, music, and dreamy moments of intimacy with your beloved. During a weekend getaway with your lover, your appetite for sensual pleasure is likely to erupt with passionate abandon. Leaving behind your practical day-to-day routines and going off for a change of scene with your partner revitalizes your love life. Even an impromptu overnight stay in a romantic setting can relieve stress and make you feel reborn.

Sexual Synergy

Virgo with Aries: Although you both value honesty and the unadorned truth, you're better at giving advice than following it. Moreover, Aries is hot tempered and outspoken, and Virgo prefers avoiding emotional scenes. Even so, the virgin is fascinated by the sexy ram's boldness and zest for living.

Virgo with Taurus: Sexually, this pair is well matched. Although the virgin may be slower to arouse, the bull has a ton of patience. With tenderness, warmth, and affection, Taurus easily melts the well-known Virgo reserve. Overall, these two Earth signs get along famously, and you two can build a rich and rewarding life together.

Virgo with Gemini: Sexually, you are on different wavelengths, but romantic Virgo can easily be swept away by fast-talking Gemini's seductive manner. Gemini is more of a risk taker and will gladly do something "just for the experience" while Virgo is more cautious and careful. Communication or miscommunication is the key to this union.

Virgo with Cancer: The relationship between this combination of Earth and Water often starts out as a friendship, and grows into a love match. Virgo is an incurable romantic, and Cancer is an absolute sucker for romance. Together you can develop a warm, loving, affectionate match, with a physical relationship that is extremely satisfying.

Virgo with Leo: Temperamentally, you two are very different. The typical Virgo is modest, self-effacing, and unobtrusive, whereas Leo craves approval, recognition, and applause. The virgin is practical, the lion extravagant. Virgo likes routine. Leo craves excitement. Nonetheless, you make a good team since each provides what the other lacks.

Virgo with Virgo: Perfectionism times two can be problematic. One possible difficulty is that Virgos are somewhat shy about lovemaking. You're more likely to flourish sexually with a bolder bedmate. Still, each one is caring and able to understand the other. Over the long term, this match can be tense, yet gratifying.

Virgo with Libra: Virgo is attracted to Libra's charm and intelligence, and Libra relates to the virgin's mental agility. Sexually, this match can work, because you both value good taste and discretion in the bedroom.

Even so, you're very different. The virgin is much more exacting in all areas of life than the easygoing, relaxed scales.

Virgo with Scorpio: Earth and Water get along well in most things, but in the sexual sphere modest Virgo may be a bit overwhelmed by Scorpio's lusty sensuality. A lot depends on the Scorpio partner's approach to lovemaking. Ultimately the virgin may be secretly thrilled by Scorpio's attempts to entice him or her into bolder sexual adventures.

Virgo with Sagittarius: Despite common interests, the energies of these two signs don't mesh well. You make a good working team because Virgo has an eye for small detail, while Sagittarius sees the larger picture. You're both romantic, but sexual compatibility may depend upon the uninhibited archer's ability to coax the virgin out of his or her shell.

Virgo with Capricorn: Both of you tend to be reserved and reluctant to express your deepest feelings. Moreover, neither of these two practical, down-to-earth signs is likely to admit to frivolous thoughts and romantic ideals. Yet you both need affection, and you're a lot more interested in the physical and emotional side of life than you let on.

Virgo with Aquarius: Natives of these two very different signs are often great friends, and under the right circumstances can be a great deal more. A love match between this unusual duo can result in a happy union, because each is rational and cerebral, and lives to learn (and teach) new things.

Virgo with Pisces: There is often a strong attraction between these two opposite signs. Since each admires certain qualities in the other, your differences tend to balance out. Pisces is a warm, generous lover who can sense the virgin's desires, and the reserved Virgo is swiftly captivated by Pisces' unrestrained sensuality.

Sun in Libra

Symbolized by the scales, Libra is a dual sign, which means that its natives generally have two distinctly different sides to their personalities. A born diplomat, you're so intent on promoting peace and harmony that you go out of your way to avoid any type of conflict. However, Libra is also known as the sign of "the iron fist in the velvet glove." Despite your reluctance to incur hassles and disagreements, you're surprisingly strong willed and rarely accept "no" for an answer. Instead of fighting, you employ your intellect, wit, and charm to subtly cajole people into doing what you want.

The representative of culture and refinement, Libra is considered the most civilized of the zodiacal signs. The typical individual born under this sign is refined, with excellent taste, delicate sensibilities, and an innate dislike of anything or anyone boorish, crude, or vulgar. Born under an Air sign, many Librans are drawn to literature, mathematics, science, and the study of human relations.

Librans generally prefer collaboration and team projects to working alone. In your personal life, you need love and companionship, and you're not likely to be truly happy without a partner. Since communication is important to you, you want your significant other to understand where you're coming from, and you'll spend hours trying to get him or her to recognize your point of view.

In Bed

Sex is a mental activity for Air signs. The patient and caring Libran's quick wit and fluency with language makes words your most powerful means of seduction; you particularly enjoy foreplay that includes plenty of suggestive conversation. A little erotica goes a long way with you, especially if it is presented in a luxurious setting. Your ideal lover has a slow, skillful touch that draws out your hidden passions and desires.

Librans believe in giving their all for love, and your romantic idealism can make you feel vulnerable in an intimate union. Disloyalty or disaffection upsets your emotional equilibrium, and if you're let down by your lover you may become seriously distressed. Since those born under the sign of the scales prefer to avoid conflict, they often display a greater tolerance for putting up with problem partners than the members of most of the other zodiacal signs.

In bed and out, you dislike hurting anyone's feelings. Although you enjoy debating and discussing things, you abhor quarrels and will rarely be caught displaying anger in an overt fashion. When you care for someone, you're unusually generous with flattery and compliments. However, you also like to be on the receiving end of flattering remarks. Like the natives of other air signs, you typically feel more through your thoughts than your emotions. For you, a truly successful intimate union requires a delicate balance of body, heart, and mind.

Turn-ons & Turn-offs

A wise partner knows how to whet your appetite for lovemaking with subtle flirting and mildly provocative suggestions. You get off on the sensual accoutrements of romance, such as sultry nightwear, silky sheets, and soft music. A few whispered words of desire speak volumes to you. Your lifelong fantasy of romantic courtship and ideal love inclines toward elegant sex, with nothing crude or tacky to offend your good taste and delicate sensibilities.

Because you're seeking perfection, you can create a bliss-filled fantasy in your mind that often seems more real than anything in the world around you. Your ideal lover discovers the details of your dream scenario and acts them out with you. Together you devise new ways of sharing and increasing your sensual pleasure. Since balance is important to you, you yearn for an intimate union with just the right degree of give and take. Making love helps you to feel complete, and you're capable of putting your own needs on hold in order to please or accommodate your lover.

Although there is little truly wild or abandoned in Libra's nature, erotic teasing acts as an enticing turn-on that adds spice and heightens your sexual ecstasy. A sexy striptease, deep enticing kisses, and languid stroking with a feather raise your temperature to a fever pitch. The thought of using sex toys may shock you, but artfully employed they intensify your lovemaking. Your brain is your most sensitive erogenous zone, and talking about sex and reading erotic literature with your lover turns you on, as does trying the sexy stuff you've been reading about and discussing.

Sexual Synergy

Libra with Aries: The natural chemistry between Libra and Aries is exceptionally strong, and your sex life should be pleasurable and mutually rewarding. But Libra wants partnership, and Aries demands freedom. Moreover, the ram usually makes up his or her mind in the blink of an eye, whereas Libra hems and haws before deciding.

Libra with Taurus: Airy Libra is drawn to the bull's earthy stability, and Taurus is captivated by the scales relaxed charm and fun-loving nature. You both seek peace and harmony, and tend to avoid conflict as much as possible. Still, beneath the smooth facade, Taurus is basically a homebody, while Libra is more of a social butterfly.

Libra with Gemini: Indecision reigns when Libra and Gemini get together, since Librans can't make up their minds, and the twins are constantly changing theirs. Nevertheless, this is an excellent match-up.

You two will laugh, talk, and make love all night long, with virtually no jealousy or possessiveness to spoil your fun and games.

Libra with Cancer: Both are sociable, but Libra tends to focus on humanity in general, while Cancer is focused on home and family. The scales are also more detached than the clinging crab, and in danger of feeling suffocated by Cancer's possessiveness. Moreover, Cancer requires considerably more attention and emotional support than Libra can give.

Libra with Leo: Each of you possesses a loving, affectionate nature with an artistic temperament. The lion is enchanted by the scales' charm and tact, and Libra loves Leo's strength and dependability. This can be a remarkably fine match, as long as the Libra partner acknowledges Leo as king or queen of his or her jungle.

Libra with Virgo: Virgo tends to see Libra as indecisive and too easygoing, while the scales may view the virgin as a prim stick-in-the-mud. The real problem between these two often comes from Libra's self-indulgent ways and love of luxury, which can drive the serious, ultra responsible Virgo straight up a wall.

Libra with Libra: The attraction between these two can be unusually strong, with lots of laughter, fun, and socializing. At first, it may seem that you are perfectly compatible and have so much in common that you feel like soul mates. But, this pairing often runs into difficulty when harsh reality intrudes on your idealistic dream of the perfect relationship.

Libra with Scorpio: There is a lot of physical magnetism between these two, yet the relationship can run into major difficulties. The scorpion is down-to-earth, ardent, and extremely jealous, whereas Libra tends to be easygoing, romantic, and flirtatious. Scorpio's passion and possessiveness may too strong for Libra to tolerate.

Libra with Sagittarius: Sexually, you're well matched, despite the fact that the romantic Libra generally prefers a less direct approach than the frank, fiery Sagittarius is capable of providing. Libra is partnership minded, and the archer is fiercely independent. Still it's a nice match-up, because you two enjoy each other's company.

Libra with Capricorn: Libra is very sociable and prefers a lifestyle that involves lots of interaction with others. Capricorn is more concerned with career, family, and practical affairs. Despite some personality conflicts, you two do have traits in common. Although Capricorn is typically more physically passionate than Libra, the Libra partner is readily seduced by a show of affection—and a touch of romance.

Libra with Aquarius: Relationship-minded Libra may view the quirky Aquarian as too independent and Bohemian, and the water bearer can find the scales' hesitancy and indecision annoying. Even so, these two Air signs have a great deal in common. You both tend to live in your minds, and need mates who are mentally alive.

Libra with Pisces: Although Air and Water don't mix well, this combination can work out beautifully. Each is basically kind, considerate, and sympathetic, and cares about people's problems. While the devoted fish may fulfill the scales' need to be adored and admired, Libra's emotional detachment could disappoint the emotionally needy Pisces.

Sun in Scorpio

Represented by the scorpion, an animal that hides in dark places and inflicts a painful sting on its enemies when threatened, the eighth sign is the most feared, misunderstood, and maligned in the zodiacal family.

More concerned with feelings than appearances, Scorpio responds to the world through emotion, based on the control and understanding of human feelings and the role they play in life. As a member of this mysterious, enigmatic sign, your immeasurable curiosity prompts you to probe, poke, and prod the depths of experience to discover what lies beneath the surface. You have a way of penetrating other people's psyches in order to ferret out their hidden agendas, while keeping your plans to yourself.

The scorpion lives in a black-and-white world of fixed ideas and opinions. On the surface you come off as easygoing, congenial, and gregarious, but underneath you're stubborn and impervious to changes not of your own making. Inherently secretive, you have your own way of doing things, and even those close to you may have difficulty understanding your true motivation.

Your perplexing ways make you hard to live with, but you're fiercely loyal to those you love. When you make a commitment, you stick to it, and don't run out on your pals at the first sign of trouble. Your capacity for stringent self-control makes you the perfect person to call on in a crisis. Smart, competent, persistent, and determined, you accomplish anything you set your mind to.

In Bed

The quintessential Scorpio struggle is that of attaining mastery over desire. Despite the sign's standing as the epitome of smoldering sexuality, the typical scorpion is capable of sublimating strong physical and emotional desires when it suits. More than the members of any other sign, Scorpios understand the power wielded by sexual overindulgence. However, you also understand the power of celibacy, and at times may alternate between periods of intense sexual activity and total abstinence.

In the bedroom, no one is as passionate as a Scorpio, and its members have well deserved reputations as enthusiastic, prodigious lovers. Your attitude toward sex and love is likely to be "all or nothing." You need to feel that you are the one in charge of your own destiny. This can be problematic, because you have a tendency to become consumed by your feelings and desires. You're not above using sex as a means of manipulating and controlling your partner, if you believe that you're losing control over your love life.

When you're in love with someone, your passionate intensity takes your partner's breath away. Despite your possessiveness, you're sympathetic, understanding, intuitive, and capable of deep love and long lasting devotion. As a Scorpio, you transform those around you, but for the most part, the person in love with you must be prepared to accept you as you are because he or she will not be able to change you.

Turn-ons & Turn-offs

The red-hot sex drive and physical prowess of Scorpios is legendary. You possess a lusty libido, and thoroughly enjoy giving and receiving sensual pleasure. Any lover stepping into your lair had better be well prepared, because keeping up with you between the sheets is an absolute must.

You require a lot of drama and emotional excitement in your love life; an intimate relationship that is too peaceful bores you. The scorpion's fascination with sex inspires numerous exotic fantasies of sultry seduction. Acting out these sexy scenarios with your bedmate is a guaranteed turn-on. Since Scorpio's fantasies are often darkly erotic, a bit of mystery or a hint of danger whets your appetite and gets your motor humming. Something of an extremist by nature, you tend to equate lovemaking with power and control. With your lover in the role of obliging love slave, you revel in the ecstatic gratification of all your secret wishes and desires—and if your partner just happens to bring along sex toys and gadgets, so much the better.

Scorpio responds to an uninhibited bed partner who entices with provocative verbal suggestions and teasing sexual games. Your sensuous nature makes any kind of massage an erotic experience for you. It can serve as arousing foreplay for steamy lovemaking, taking you to the very edge of intense sensual pleasure. However, a loving, aromatic massage may also kindle your physical desire so strongly that you feel as though you can't delay sexual gratification a moment longer. Since Scorpio is the most sexually charged of all zodiac signs, your nether regions are extremely sensitive. Any stimulation down below gets you incredibly aroused. Consequently, many a Scorpio bedroom massage has to be abandoned halfway though.

Sexual Synergy

Scorpio with Aries: Sexually, you're well matched, because each of you is imaginative, passionate, ardent, and energetic. Since neither is bound by convention, you're adventurous and willing to experiment sexually. Even so, Scorpio's possessiveness and jealousy can drive the happy-go-lucky, independent ram up the wall.

Scorpio with Taurus: When the jealous scorpion and the possessive bull come together, the union can turn into an ongoing battle. Despite the strong physical attraction, you can only achieve harmony through the exercise of tolerance and patience on both sides. If you overcome your differences, you may forge a bond strong enough to last a lifetime.

Scorpio with Gemini: A difficult combination. Scorpio is intense and emotional. Gemini is cool and easygoing. Scorpio has a jealous nature and Gemini can be quite fickle; if the scorpion holds the reigns too tightly, the twins might bolt. Still, the twins may find the scorpion's sexual aura compelling. Gemini enjoys differences. Scorpio does not.

Scorpio with Cancer: The attraction between these two Water signs is typically strong and immediate. Because you two connect on so many levels, the chances of a long-lasting relationship are excellent. Still, there are some possible pitfalls along your road to happiness. Each of you is jealous, with a tendency to see rivals even when none exist.

Scorpio with Leo: The immediate and intense sexual attraction between these two often gives rise to an "all or nothing" relationship. Sunny Leo is outgoing and open, whereas the scorpion is complex and secretive. To Leo, Scorpio seems devious and manipulative, while Scorpio is likely to resent the lion's attempts to dominate the union.

Scorpio with Virgo: Scorpio's possessiveness scares Virgo, but it also gives the virgin a strong sense of being loved and protected. Virgo's propensity for handing out unsolicited advice does not sit well with Scorpio, and if these two are to get along Virgo must realize that the scorpion won't put up with nagging or criticism.

Scorpio with Libra: In this union, Scorpio leads the way in most things, and gentle Libra appears to follow. However, Librans usually find a way of getting others (even intractable scorpions) to do their bidding. Cardinal Air and Fixed Water have little in common. Yet, if this relationship can get past the initial courtship, it may very well last a lifetime.

Scorpio with Scorpio: A love match between two scorpions can be interesting, and you two actually get along surprisingly well together. You're able to read each other's minds, and have the same likes and dislikes. Problems may arise if either of you tries to run the show. Shared power and responsibility is the only way for a happy union.

Scorpio with Sagittarius: It's pure sexual attraction at first sight when the archer and the scorpion meet. But Scorpio cools down pretty fast when hit with the realization that Sagittarius is just out for fun and games. The freewheeling archer won't stand for Scorpio's jealousy, whereas Scorpio views Sagittarius' flighty ways as acts of disloyalty.

Scorpio with Capricorn: Sexually, you're very well matched. Even so, Scorpio feels things deeply, and Capricorn is cool and unemotional. Both are ambitious and each likes being in charge, so your powerful personalities may clash. However, this union works, because you two understand each other better than most.

Scorpio with Aquarius: Airy, absent-minded, freedom-loving Aquarius and intense, possessive Scorpio make an odd couple. Yet, despite all your differences (or perhaps because of them), Scorpio and Aquarius often find each other totally fascinating, and a successful love affair or even marriage between you is possible.

Scorpio with Pisces: Both Scorpio and Pisces are sensitive, feeling, and compassionate individuals, and together you have a depth of intimacy and emotional union that you will find with few others. Moreover, you share a deep psychic link that typifies true soul mates. This is a good match, as long as you can put up with each other's dark moods.

Sun in Sagittarius

The archer is the eternal wanderer and truth-seeker of the zodiac, a free spirit whose gaze is perpetually fixed on the far horizon. Knowledge and freedom are the touchstones of your existence, because they help you transcend the petty limitations that others readily accept. At home in the outdoors and on the open road, you love to travel and meet new people. You view life as a search for experience and adventure, a journey in which the voyage itself is infinitely more important than the destination.

Straightforward, trusting, and everyone's pal, the archer is one of the nicest friends anyone could have. You're willing to do favors for people and offer your help with no strings attached. While neither possessive nor jealous of your partner's other relationships, true intimacy is not your thing. You value your freedom and grant the same to others. Your inclination to constantly rush off in search of new experiences gives you an elusive quality that keeps people at arm's length.

Sagittarians rarely meddle in anyone else's affairs, unless specifically asked for advice. Nevertheless, when your opinion is requested, you have all the answers. Famous for their foot-in-the-mouth brand of honesty, archers don't know how to beat around the bush. Incapable of malice, your blunt comments are never made out of spite. If your outspoken remarks hurt someone's feelings, you're truly sorry.

In Bed

Sagittarians make charming, charismatic lovers who are affectionate, straightforward, and sincere. Someone out for a good time need look no further than a Sagittarius, because in bed no other sign is as sexy or as much fun. Although most archers are strongly sexed, what they really care about is friendship and the *experience* of love. Whereas the youthful archer may become involved in steamy affairs with several different partners, the older Sagittarius often settles down with one person. Later on in life, some natives of this Sun sign seem to forget about sex altogether, especially if their attention is totally focused on interesting work or an engaging project or hobby.

The fiery archer is inherently more physical and intellectual than emotional. Where lovemaking is concerned, you're definitely not shy. Like the half beast/half human that your Sun sign represents, you're quite the sexual animal. Freewheeling and open-minded, you immerse yourself in the erotic experience. You're willing to try anything at least once. In bed, mental stimulation can be as exciting to you as the sexual kind, especially if the conversation is honest and open. You need a bed partner you can talk to. While intellectual compatibility is very important, Sagittarians are not snobs, and differences in social backgrounds or ethnic origins don't matter to you.

The typical archer views sex as something to enjoy and not take too seriously. In your view, the real bond between lovers comes from sharing all the wonderful things that life offers. Your ideal lover is not only as ardent and free-spirited as you are, but is capable of engaging you in a lively conversation on diverse subjects, while making love to you in various and sundry sexual positions.

Turn-ons & Turn-offs

Sagittarians relish the thrill of the chase. Once a relationship starts settling down, the archer strives to keep things exciting. Above all, you want to have a good time with your beloved. Although you express your sexual feelings easily and passionately, when the sex is over you want to move on to something else. You're not into twenty-four–hour togetherness, but you thoroughly enjoy doing interesting things with your partner, particularly outside in the open air. Sharing physical activities such as dancing or working out together gets you pumped up for lovemaking. You also enjoy sex "alfresco." Under the stars, the boardwalk, or the bleachers, you're turned on by the carefree abandon of following your impulses, wherever they may lead.

Although disinterested in emotional game playing, you do enjoy being seduced by sexy attire and other exotic enhancements to sensual pleasure. Spicy sexual banter liberates your quick wit and increases your anticipation of the sensual delights to follow. Fooling around with sex toys and naughty novelties stirs your imagination and energizes your libido. Erotic bedroom fun is your ultimate turn-on, and seductive teasing and touching wakens your desire and heightens the ensuing ecstasy. Since Sagittarius is associated with the hips and thighs, light stroking of your inner thigh inflames all your erogenous zones.

Sexual Synergy

Sagittarius with Aries: It's nonstop fun when the archer and ram get together. You two have so much in common that you probably feel like soul mates. Still, Aries may consider the outspoken archer's blunt remarks too candid and the easygoing Sagittarius can have difficulty with the ram's hot temper and domineering ways.

Sagittarius with Taurus: These two march to different drummers. Sagittarius needs excitement and freedom, while Taurus demands safety and security. Where the archer is active and impulsive, the bull is slow and controlled. Although a fiery sexual relationship helps soften your differences, this combination only works if you both agree to make concessions.

Sagittarius with Gemini: Since these opposite signs are so much alike, there's often an instant physical and mental attraction. Both are sociable, intellectual, athletic, and adore travel. Because each is restless and freedom-oriented, with a relaxed attitude toward relationships, you two may ultimately wander off in separate directions.

Sagittarius with Cancer: The crab and the archer make an odd combination, yet often find themselves strongly attracted to each other. Watery Cancer wants a permanent union with a settled home life, while fiery

Sagittarius craves excitement, freedom, and adventure. Still, both like to travel, and Sagittarius enjoys the comforts Cancer provides at home.

Sagittarius with Leo: These fiery signs usually get along famously—in the bedroom and elsewhere. Both are passionate, openhearted, and cheerful. Sagittarius won't resent the lion's need to shine, and Leo is too busy to envy the archer's popularity. When Sagittarius allows the lion to rule, it's fun and excitement times two for this near perfect match-up.

Sagittarius with Virgo: A love match between a Sagittarius and a Virgo is unlikely, but not impossible. The virgin focuses on the trees, whereas the archer is interested in the forest. While these different approaches may balance each other, they can also cause conflict. Tolerance and understanding of your differences are required for this to work.

Sagittarius with Libra: You two have a lot in common, and can be great pals as well as lovers. Each is friendly, outgoing, and exceedingly sociable, but the cultured scales love beauty and luxury, while the athletic archer is more the rugged outdoorsy type. Problems may arise because Librans tend to think in pairs, and archers prize freedom above all else.

Sagittarius with Scorpio: Sagittarius is intrigued by Scorpio's magnetic sexual intensity. Scorpio, however, cannot quite comprehend the archer's fun-and-games approach to life and love. When the open, jovial Sagittarius tries getting close to the brooding, secretive scorpion, the archer may become disenchanted and go skipping off to the nearest party.

Sagittarius with Sagittarius: Although this combination makes for a super-exciting, exhilarating rollercoaster ride, once the fun stops you two may drift apart. A double dose of restless independence can be too hectic and unstable for either of you. At least one archer should be capable of handling practical matters, while the other goes out to play.

Sagittarius with Capricorn: This is a difficult, but not totally impossible combination that works best if each partner is willing to accept the other without trying to change him or her. Sexually, the fiery archer is warm-blooded, passionate, and desirous, and the goat, while not overly demonstrative, is highly sexed, ardent, and responsive.

Sagittarius with Aquarius: These two usually fall in "like" at first sight, and can be great buddies as well as lovers. Your shared curiosity and adventurous spirits extend to the bedroom, where the lovemaking is uninhibited, and full of fun. While your temperaments and interests may be somewhat different, they blend together well.

Sagittarius with Pisces: Sagittarius is readily captivated by ethereal Pisces' aura of mystery. Pisces is typically attracted to the archer's magnetic personality and vibrant self-assurance. However, a long-term relationship between you two can be problematic. Fish are needy and possessive, and Sagittarians resent restrictions on their personal freedom.

Sun in Capricorn

Capricorn natives are the workers and builders of our society. An exceptional planner, organizer, and strategist, you're prepared to do whatever you deem necessary to attain your goals. Moreover, you're patient, and willing to wait however long it takes. Your determination and refusal to quit, no matter what the circumstances, virtually guarantee that you will get what you go after. Even when you're knocked down along the way, you bounce right back up again.

Your private side is very different from your public image. You're rarely as relaxed in society as you are in career situations. You always seem to find something to fret about and you often wonder if there is something important that you've forgotten to do. Your feelings run deep, but most of the time you keep them hidden beneath a protective shell. Cool and self-contained, it takes you a while to warm up and allow someone new into your life. But anyone who cares enough to try and penetrate your shell is greatly rewarded. Your affections and loyalties are strong, and you cherish your close friends as much as your family.

In Bed

Capricorn actually ranks among the most strongly sexed of the zodiacal signs and, where ardor and sexual prowess are concerned, many goats could give Aries and Scorpio a run for the money. The typical Capricorn is extremely sensual, but while goats need love more than most, they often have great difficulty expressing their desires.

In Capricorn, the carnal appetite of the Earth signs and the assertive nature of the Cardinal signs come together to produce some very horny goats. Although there are some emotional inhibitions, with the right partner your innate sensuality comes to the forefront. Pleasure between the sheets is generally a straightforward affair for the Capricorn, who doesn't need anything flashy or fancy to arouse his or her lusty libido.

As a Capricorn you want a lover who will cherish you and understand your dark moods, without trying to get you to relinquish control over your life goals. You're realistic enough to realize that you are something of a perfectionist, and that everything you desire in a mate or partner may be hard to find. Still, you're not likely to settle for less, and are willing to wait as long as it takes for your genuine soul mate to appear. If, in the meantime, you should happen to fall in love with someone you consider unsavory or unsuitable, you'd rather say "adios" than modify your life plan.

Turn-ons & Turn-offs

Capricorns are inherently cautious and less likely to engage in casual sex than other signs. The more secure you feel in a relationship, the more likely you are to cast aside your inhibitions and follow the impulses of your sensuality. Your distaste for public displays of affection helps you keep your powerful libido under strict control outside the bedroom. Even in private, it may take some encouragement from your partner before you loosen up enough to follow your wildest carnal impulses. However, once you get going, your approach to lovemaking is lusty and straightforward.

Although basically conventional, the goat enjoys being courted and coaxed. Nothing turns you on as fast as a well-staged seduction scene with all the traditional trimmings: sexy attire, silky sheets, dim lighting, music, candles, and a properly chilled bottle of bubbly. The intensity of Capricorn's sex drive goes through cycles depending on workload and various mood swings. Your ideal lover senses your moods and intuits your shifting needs. The legs and especially the knees are very sensitive in Capricorn natives. Light stroking on the backs of your knees is guaranteed to stir your slumbering passions. During low periods, your partner may reawaken physical desire by trailing a large feather or bit of fur over your skin, especially in these ultra sensitive areas.

Although you don't normally require a lot of foreplay to get in the mood, you enjoy being caressed and pampered when you're feeling stressed. An erotic massage helps you relax and sets the stage for lovemaking. Where love and sex are concerned, goats cannot be rushed. Quickies don't really satisfy you. You prefer taking it slow–and getting it right. Endurance is Capricorn's forte. Once aroused, you can keep going all night long. You're proud of your sexual prowess, and satisfying your bedmate's needs and desires is as important to you as satisfying your own.

Sexual Synergy

Capricorn with Aries: The typical ram is vivacious and outgoing, the goat reserved and cautious. As romantic partners, you two could have some major obstacles to overcome. Although lusty Capricorn is intrigued by Aries' smoldering sex appeal, problems may arise if the possessive, domineering goat attempts to control the independent-minded ram.

Capricorn with Taurus: Taurus can be Capricorn's ideal counterpart, because there is an intuitive understanding between these two. Over time, despite both signs' strong sexual needs and desires, this earthy duo's lovemaking could fall into a bit of a rut. While neither is particularly inventive in bed, the sensual bull has ways of warming up the cooler goat.

Capricorn with Gemini: A love match between these two is unlikely, but not impossible. Although members of these two signs have little in common, staid Capricorn is fascinated by Gemini's spirited behavior. To the goat, the twins represent temptation, yet deep down, the responsible Capricorn admires freewheeling Gemini's audacity and wishes to emulate it.

Capricorn with Cancer: The crab and the goat have many of the same goals, and share a similar respect for convention and tradition. Both are physically passionate, and there's likely to be a strong sexual attraction. Problems that arise are almost always emotional. Cancer is openly affectionate, whereas Capricorn is cooler and more reserved

Capricorn with Leo: A love match between Capricorn and Leo can be quite interesting. The dramatic, flamboyant lion loves having a good time. Yet the goat is more practical, and wary of too much self-indulgence. Even so, both are strongly sexed, goal-oriented, and focused on success. This combo works, as long as neither tries to control the other.

Capricorn with Virgo: There is often a strong attraction between Virgo and Capricorn. These signs tend to be reserved and reluctant to express their deepest feelings, yet both long for love and approval. If these two can learn how to relax and trust, they may forge a bond of true intimacy.

Capricorn with Libra: Members of these two Cardinal signs are more likely to be drawn together as business partners than lovers. Still, there is often a strong physical attraction, and the possibility of a romance cannot be discounted. Capricorn is intrigued by Libra's magnetic charm, while Libra admires the goat's driving ambition.

Capricorn with Scorpio: These two signs have a great deal in common and understand each other better than most. Both are careful about revealing true feelings, and it takes time for each to trust and open up emotionally. Sexually, you're well matched, but where Scorpio feels things very deeply, Capricorn is cool and unemotional.

Capricorn with Sagittarius: The question here is whether Capricorn can deal with Sagittarius' lighthearted approach to life, and whether the archer can put up with the goat's controlling ways. Even so, this union may work. The goat grounds the flighty archer, and Sagittarius injects excitement into the goat's humdrum existence.

Capricorn with Capricorn: Sexually, this should be a good match, because Capricorns typically possess well-developed sexual appetites. Nevertheless, two serious, responsible goats may forget to have fun. Still, nobody understands one goat as well as another one. Once you settle the power and control issues, you two can build a lasting relationship.

Capricorn with Aquarius: At best, this is a difficult match-up. Capricorn is conventional, and Aquarius a born rebel. The water bearer demands freedom to come and go without questions or restrictions, and this trait doesn't sit well with the possessive goat. A considerable amount of tolerance and understanding is required for this union to work.

Capricorn with Pisces: At first glance it may seem as though the goat and the fish don't have much in common, but these two actually have a great deal to offer each other. Sexually, your relationship should be close and satisfying, in spite of the fact that Pisces may sometimes wish that the goat was a bit more romantic and emotionally accessible.

Sun in Aquarius

The individualistic, unconventional water bearer possesses an elusive quality that's difficult to define. Although some members of this sign are inherently eccentric, others seem to deliberately cultivate eccentricity as a lifestyle. With such a paradoxical nature, there's really no such thing as a typical Aquarian. You're an individualist who is often involved with groups, a loner who hates being alone. Because of Aquarius's Fixed quality, you can be headstrong and inflexible, and your airy nature may make you appear aloof and impersonal. A born rebel, you confront the world on your own terms. You truly enjoy being different, and if something you do or say shocks people, so much the better.

Intellectually and technologically oriented, Aquarians are most comfortable in the company of people who share their unusual interests and ideas. With a head crammed full of thoughts and ideas about tomorrow, forward-looking Aquarius has difficulty staying focused in the here and now.

Close relationships are important to you, but casual acquaintances are easier for you to sustain than intimate ones. A genuine humanitarian, you believe everyone is equal. Yet, even though you care about the welfare of the world, your air of detachment makes you appear unapproachable. Your desire for independence causes you to shy away from any relationship where your freedom may be compromised.

In Bed

Aquarians are open to suggestion and generally willing to experiment in the bedroom. As an intellectual, your initial reactions to things are more cerebral than physical. Aquarius is not especially sentimental or romantic, but water bearers are super idealistic. The person interested in winning your love can skip the moonlight, flowers, and poetry. However, if he or she betrays your trust in any way, you're not likely to forgive or forget. On a physical level Aquarians tend to be low key, letting the other person take the initiative. However, any approach needs to be subtle and tactful. You can be coaxed and seduced, but you refuse to be dominated. Romantically, you're something of a slow starter, but once you get going you make a passionate, imaginative, enthusiastic, and considerate lover. Your natural curiosity encourages you to experiment with creative ideas, in bed and out. There is a delightfully sexual being lurking beneath your cool intellectual demeanor, and the lover who recognizes this is in for a wild ride indeed. Despite this, some part of your emotional nature is always held in reserve, so you never totally lose either your head—or your heart.

Turn-ons & Turn-offs

As befits an Air sign, Aquarians approach sex mentally as well as physically. Your bedroom antics are greatly enhanced when you're able to share your thoughts and ideas with your lover. Your natural curiosity inclines toward creative experimentation between the sheets. A delicious eroticism lurks beneath the surface of your outwardly controlled manner, and the partner who is able to tap into it can look forward to good times in your bed.

Physically you are strongly sexed and passionate. However, your mind is easily distracted, which can cause you to ignore the needs and desires of your body. When this happens, a few verbal reminders of the delights you are missing are all it takes to inflame your lusty libido. Because your mind and imagination are your major erotic zones, you respond as readily to spoken intentions as to physical stimulation. Since you enjoy a bit of fun mixed in with your lovemaking, you like being with a bedmate who amuses you. Stylized role-playing fantasies and sex games can add a touch of spice and glamour to your love life.

Aquarius can be wildly passionate one night, yet seemingly disinterested the next. The romantic fantasy that got your sexual juices flowing last night may have the opposite effect today. Aquarians are generally freewheeling, open-minded, and sexually liberated. Yet, despite that touch of kinkiness in your makeup, you truly dislike outright vulgarity. Whereas hashing over your lustful intentions with your lover is a genuine turn-on, you're turned off by really crude or raunchy behavior.

Sexual Synergy

Aquarius with Aries: True friendship and tolerance of idiosyncrasies form the basis of this relationship, even in its most passionate moments. You both love freedom and adventure, and can enjoy being together without trying to tie each other down. Problems may arise if Aries gets bossy, because Aquarius refuses to be dominated.

Aquarius with Taurus: If the choice of a lover was ruled by the head instead of the heart, neither of these Fixed signs is likely to be the other's first pick. The bull wants material things, and the water bearer is far more interested in ideas. Even so Taurus is intrigued by Aquarius's unconventionality and is interested in seeing where it can lead.

Aquarius with Gemini: This pairing often begins with a harmonious companionship that eventually grows into love. Even if the romantic relationship ends, these two airy partners are almost always able to salvage their friendship. The only real problem with this match-up is that both Gemini and Aquarius tend to be erratic and unlikely to commit.

Aquarius with Cancer: A love match between this pair can be difficult and requires a lot of compromise. Each is of you is caring, giving, and compassionate, albeit in different ways. Cancer's possessiveness makes the freedom-loving water bearer uncomfortable, and Aquarius's inability to respond to emotional needs is guaranteed to upset the sensitive crab.

Aquarius with Leo: With Leo and Aquarius there is no hidden agenda—what you see is what you get! However, your initial attraction to each other may be nipped in the bud if the water bearer insists on analyzing the lion's actions and decisions. Or if Leo tries to dominate, since no one can tell the fiercely independent Aquarian what to do.

Aquarius with Virgo: Temperamentally you're very different, but on a mental level you're both cerebral and analytical. Virgo delights in efficiency and order and may find the water bearer's chaotic approach to life somewhat unnerving. Even so, a match between you two can result in a happy union if you're able to confront your problems in a rational manner.

Aquarius with Libra: Each of you is extremely friendly and sociable, while remaining somewhat detached emotionally. Libra is focused on partnership and dislikes spending time alone, while Aquarius is independent and needs some space. However, you two can resolve most of your differences by talking them through.

Aquarius with Scorpio: Scorpio is the most controlling sign, and Aquarius is the least controllable. Whereas the scorpion is super emotional, the water bearer is cool-headed and logical. Yet Aquarius finds

Scorpio's compelling magnetism alluring, and the sexy scorpion is often fascinated by the quirky water bearer's freewheeling Bohemianism.

Aquarius with Sagittarius: Although the fiery archer may not understand the water bearer's remoteness, the intense mental connection between you usually makes up for any lack of emotional intimacy. Your shared curiosity and adventurous spirits extend to the bedroom, where the lovemaking is sure to be imaginative, uninhibited, and full of fun.

Aquarius with Capricorn: Both the goat and the water bearer are physically responsive, yet emotionally cool. Aquarius is a rebel; Capricorn is conventional. Still, a curious fascination can arise between you. Aquarius cherishes independence and may prefer friendship to commitment, but the goat can be persuasive.

Aquarius with Aquarius: Sexually, you two are well matched. Although not as passionate as some, as lovers you're inventive and open-minded. You know how to stimulate each other mentally and physically and, while your emotional temperatures may be a bit cooler than those of other couples, the bond of loyalty between you is stronger than most.

Aquarius with Pisces: It can be difficult for you two to satisfy each other's needs. Pisces demands attention and proof of love, when all Aquarius wants is to be left alone. Sexually, the sensuous fish projects an air of mystery that fascinates the water bearer, but the spell can be easily broken if your intimate moments turn into an emotional tug of war.

Sun in Pisces

Pisces' reputation as one of the most perplexing and difficult signs to understand is well deserved. They are like chameleons that change color to match their surroundings. The intriguing combination of the Water element and the Mutable quality gives you your special gift—your ability to fit in no matter where you happen to be. The symbol for your sign—a pair of fish swimming in opposite directions—emphasizes the basic duality of your nature. It sometimes seems as though you're several different personalities rolled into one. As a result, you get along famously with all types of people. The aura of mystery that surrounds you comes as much from the fish's innate talent for changing in manner and appearance in the blink of an eye, as well as from your own inclination to keep your dreams and secrets to yourself.

Intuitive Pisces relates to the world through emotions rather than physical action or intellect. You're a romantic to the core and feel empty and incomplete without love in your life. Your understanding of intimate relationships is so strongly influenced by your dreams and ideals that you tend to believe people actually are whatever you fervently wish them to be. Compassionate, kind, and loving, you could be an easy mark for a good sob story. However, despite a seemingly fragile psyche and a dislike of confrontation, fish are actually a lot tougher than most people realize. Pisces is no patsy and, when you need help or support, you're not above using a charming, indirect approach that appeals to your lover's protective nature and eventually gets you what you want.

In Bed

Although fish are not normally sexually aggressive, they're among the most beguiling and alluring individuals in the zodiac. You don't need to pursue love, because love generally has a way of finding you. Fish often come off as shy and quiet in public, but in the privacy of the bedroom, you blossom into a sensual and creative lover, adoring both playful and passionate sexual encounters with your partner.

In bed, you like to combine the real and surreal, so your lovemaking becomes a creative hyperstate where most anything is possible. If your lover is the type who enjoys indulging in role-playing games or other flights of erotic fancy, you're primed to go all night long. As with so much of your life, love and sex is a magical tour of mind, body, and soul. Pisces possesses a kind of sexual electricity that is almost magnetic, and this mysterious quality works as an aphrodisiac in the game of love.

Sex as a complete spiritual and physical union makes you feel safe, free, and uninhibited. Naturally kind and compassionate, the act of pleasing your partner is second nature, in and out of bed. You give of yourself repeatedly, without expecting anything in return. You love completely, and view this sacred state as the best that life has to offer. Love can be particularly scary for the fish, yet when it's right, it has the power to transcend all limits and transport you to a new world.

Turn-ons & Turn-offs

Sex for you is a beautiful fantasy in which you merge and blend with your partner to become one soul. The lover who inflames your imagination is the one most likely to set your libido on fire. Just gazing into his or her eyes doesn't quite do it for you. You crave romance with a capital *R*. A romantic getaway for two is often the first step toward making your erotic dreams reality.

You respond enthusiastically to lovemaking in a dreamy location, preferably one on or near a body of water. It doesn't really matter if it's a luxurious cruise or a single night at Budget Beach. Even at home, nothing turns you on like a sensuous bath or a spa soak with your beloved. Afterward, you like being toweled dry and dusted with powder like a baby. The feet are Pisces' major erogenous zone. Most enjoy having their feet held, bathed, stroked, and massaged, and toe sucking drives them into a sensual frenzy.

Pisces' sexual cravings can be somewhat unpredictable, and often encompass a wide range of erotic fantasies. Driven by emotions as well as physical desire, you crave a bit of drama in the boudoir. When you get bored you may yearn for a dream lover to come and whisk you off to some wild and exotic love nest. Barring this, you get off on the fun and excitement of fantasy-inspired sex games. The lover who is able to surprise you with something new or different in the bedroom will continue to hold your interest. You are particularly fond of little presents, especially if the gifts are seductive garments or sex toys designed to increase pleasure and excitement.

Sexual Synergy

Pisces with Aries: Pisces is a sensitive dreamer, Aries an aggressive doer. Pisces' idea of a romantic date may be a night at the opera, while the ram would rather go to a basketball game. However, each is caring, idealistic, and romantic. If Pisces is willing to feed the ram's ego, you two should get along okay.

Pisces with Taurus: Both are ultimate romantics, and share a deep appreciation for beauty, art, and music. Although dreamy Pisces may sometimes try the bull's famous patience, you two have much to give each other. As long as Pisces is caring and attentive, the bull is usually willing to overlook the inevitable differences.

Pisces with Gemini: These two Mutable signs have some interests in common, but their differing temperaments make this an uncertain match-up. Gemini may be captivated by the elusive fish's air of mystery, but has little patience with Pisces' emotional outbursts. The twin's cool indifference can drive the needy, ultrasensitive fish straight up the wall.

Pisces with Cancer: This is a very compatible combination. You two feel safe together, because you're tuned to the same wavelength and are able to protect each other's feelings. However, both are extremely sensitive. When hurt or disappointed, the crab crawls off to hide in his or her shell and brood in silence, whereas the emotional fish collapses in tears.

Pisces with Leo: Leo and Pisces often find themselves attracted to each other, precisely because they are so different. The fish is fascinated by Leo's dramatic persona, and the lion is intrigued by Pisces' mystical aura. Still, before long, flamboyant Leo begins to grate on the fish's nerves, and Pisces' moodiness gives the lion cause to bolt for the exit.

Pisces with Virgo: Virgo is cerebral, reserved, and fault finding. Pisces is super emotional and easily hurt. Even so, Pisces finds Virgo's common-sense approach to life comforting. Pisces is a warm, generous lover, capable of sensing Virgo's moods and desires, and the naturally reserved virgin is intrigued and turned-on by the fish's unrestrained sensuality.

Pisces with Libra: You two are the classic "people who need people." Each is romantic, caring, and idealistic, and you get along well together because you both want peace and harmony. Sexually you two are compatible, but emotionally you are on different planets. Pisces' clingy nature tends to scare Libra, and the scales' cool detachment upsets the fish.

Pisces with Scorpio: The fish may sometimes feel overwhelmed by the scorpion's power and intensity, but Pisces really likes having someone to lean on. Both are moody, yet Pisces has some difficulty understanding Scorpio's need to be alone during dark times. Still, you two are genuine soul mates and share the Water signs' deep psychic connection.

Pisces with Sagittarius: A match between these two can be difficult. Although Pisces is attracted to Sagittarius' buoyant vitality, the archer's spirit can be dampened by the fish's tendency toward dependency. Archers are adventurous wanderers; fish are homebodies. When Pisces longs to spend time with Sagittarius, the archer usually has someplace to go.

Pisces with Capricorn: Despite differences in temperament, you two have a great deal to offer one other. While Capricorn is not as emotional as Pisces, the goat is protective and can be surprisingly patient when dealing with the fish's insecurities. Pisces is kind and caring, and looks up to Capricorn in a way that makes the goat feel appreciated.

Pisces with Aquarius: A successful match between these two can be difficult to achieve. Pisces is arguably the most emotional sign in the zodiac; Aquarius the least emotional one. Although each of you is a visionary who gets off on helping people, in other ways you are very different. Compromise is the best hope for this pairing.

Pisces with Pisces: As psychic soul mates, you make an outstanding team. Thanks to the innate passivity of your natures, there is sure to be little conflict when you are together. However, neither of you is focused on the practical realities of daily living. Too much alike to avoid chaos, you may require hired help to keep your domestic lives in order.

2

Mars

THE ROMAN WAR GOD, MARS, WAS ONE OF THE MOST PROMINENT and worshipped deities of the pantheon. As patron of all soldiers, Mars was extremely popular and revered throughout the empire, especially in Roman Britain. Usually portrayed as a warrior in full battle armor, no general would consider going into combat without first invoking Mars in his sanctuary. In the ancient world, wars were often started or renewed in spring, and the month of March, noted for its violent weather, was named for Mars and dedicated to him.

Closely connected to your sense of personal identity and individual level of self-sufficiency, Mars in the birth chart represents strength of will and the desire to win and conquer. The key Martian qualities are aggression, anger, confidence, courage, independence, leadership, athleticism, passion, sexuality, and masculinity. The zodiacal sign Mars occupies in your horoscope shows your level of energy and how you use that energy to overcome obstacles. If you don't know your Mars sign, you can find it by looking it up in Appendix C: Mars and Venus Ephemeris Tables.

This sign also indicates your aggression type (aggressive; passive; passive aggressive) and how you use that aggression to get what you want in life. In addition, it points out those life areas where you're most likely to assert your individuality. Because Mars has so much to do with the projection of personality, its elemental position in your horoscope suggests whether your energies are going to be largely physical (Fire), material (Earth), mental (Air), or emotional (Water).

People with Mars in the Fire signs (Aries, Leo, and Sagittarius) are assertive, daring, optimistic, and impractical. Impulsive and willing to take risks, Fire signs seize both the moment and opportunity as they arise. People with Mars in the Fire signs rarely concern themselves with fortune's ups and downs, because they believe better days are coming and that they will always win out in the end.

Those with Mars in the Earth signs (Taurus, Virgo, and Capricorn) tend to equate security with worldly status, and their focus is on the accumulation of material goods. Inclined to work first and play later, earthy individuals are practical and goal-oriented. Willing to work hard, they give their all and expect tangible rewards in return.

Individuals with Mars in the Air signs (Gemini, Libra, and Aquarius) are more interested in abstract ideas and artistic concepts than in practical matters. Airy types tend to be motivated by a questing spirit and the ongoing need for communication and social interaction. They strive for intellectual independence, physical freedom, and the opportunity to use their creative imaginations in innovative ways.

People with Mars in the Water signs (Cancer, Scorpio, and Pisces) are sensitive, intuitive, changeable, impressionable, and impractical. Emotional security is their main concern, and they often equate emotional security with material security. Motivated more by feeling than logic, they sometimes go too far in following their hunches. Nevertheless, individuals with Mars in Water signs are usually able to capitalize on their intuitive understanding of people and situations.

The way Mars manifests itself in your chart is a clear indicator of the type of lovemaking you're likely to enjoy. Your Mars sign, discussed in detail below, defines what you desire, how you express that desire, and how you go about satisfying it. Mars also denotes basic survival instincts. It involves things like action, movement, and the "fight or flight" instinct.

Mars in Aries

Mars is strongest in Aries, its natural sign, where it represents high energy, courage, and initiative. Your sex drive is powerful, spontaneous, and easily awakened. In Aries, Mars is all about action and, when your passions are aroused, you rarely stop to consider possible consequences. The ultimate individualist, you cannot bear anyone telling you what to do. New people and fresh projects make you happiest. When life starts getting predictable, you get antsy. While living with you is never dull or boring, it can be difficult. Impulsive and supremely confident, you're not overly inclined to look (or think) before you leap.

The negative aspect of Mars in Aries is lack of restraint. Despite your leadership abilities you're not very good at compromise or teamwork, because you always want to do things your own way. You won't tolerate opposition or interference and, at times your Martian temper can get you into serious trouble.

Sex is best for you when it's spontaneous and unrestricted. Although sometimes aggressive in bed, you're sincere and enthusiastic in your sexual expression. Between the sheets, you can get impatient with too much foreplay, preferring to get right to the point. While other signs may be more aroused by courtship and romance, you're aroused by the sex act itself, plain and simple. Your head is your major erogenous zone, and you like having your lover massage your scalp or run fingers through your hair.

Mars in Taurus

Mars, the planet of energy, isn't very active in Taurus, and your physical drive is often reduced to a low gear. However, what you lack in aggressiveness and mobility, you make up for with outstanding endurance. When you finally get rolling in one direction, it is virtually impossible to get you to change course. Naturally patient and persistent, you simply wait for however long it takes. Mars in Taurus is inherently possessive, with a strong sense of ownership. Once you've gained your prize, no one is going to be allowed to take it away from you. Above all, you need stability and security in your love life. When you find it, you make a loyal and devoted romantic partner.

Mars in Taurus denotes a lot of practical and emotional energy. However, the physical side of life can be rather flat, and interest in the intellectual side may also be restrained. Mars in Taurus also shows a lack of flexibility. Taurus is a Fixed sign, and Martian energies normally expressed as anger can come out looking like stubbornness. Emotions that are held too tightly may later be released in a major blow up.

Sexually, Mars in Taurus is hedonistic and sensual. High on your list of life's priorities is satisfying the physical desires. Your approach to sexuality is laid back and uncomplicated without fantasies or fetishes, and is almost never rushed. Moreover, your sensuality is about more than just sex. It extends to all five senses. You respond sensuously to beauty in your surroundings, people, nature, and the arts.

Mars in Gemini

In Gemini, Martian energy is scattered and unfocused and you are prone to erratic mood swings. As long as there are lots of interesting things on your plate, you are a powerhouse of physical energy, but when there's nothing to do, you're easily exhausted. However, because this sign produces mental assertiveness, your mental energies are invariably high, which can cause airy Gemini to seem to be lacking emotionally.

Communication is very important to Gemini. The partner who stimulates you intellectually will spark your romantic and sexual interest. With your Mars in Gemini, you are especially drawn to potential lovers who pique your curiosity and offer you a variety of fresh experiences. In your world, being interesting is much more important than being physically attractive.

For you, variety is the spice of life and your sex drive is fueled by your mind as much as your body. Since your intellect is your most active erogenous zone, your style of lovemaking is playful and inventive. Gemini's preferred form of erotic communication is decidedly verbal. Typically, the sociable, vivacious, articulate individuals born under this Mars sign are incurable flirts. You eagerly pursue new interests in love and romance, and may find it difficult to remain constant to one particular partner.

Mars in Cancer

In Cancer, Martian energies are more emotional than physical or intellectual, causing you to resist change because you need to feel secure and in charge before you act. As a result, you can appear slow and weak at times. However, your strength lies in the crab's tenacity and persistence.

This placement of Mars is not very competitive, and the crab is disinclined to engage in any sort of physical or mental combat. Mars in Cancer does have an extremely positive side, as it often manifests as a quiet, peaceful, helpful nature. You possess an almost infinite ability to compassionately respond to the needs and demands of others, especially friends and family members.

Your sex drive is highly passionate, but very closely tied to your emotional needs. In an intimate situation, you must feel safe and secure before letting go. When you do, your responses are extremely intense and seductive. With encouragement and reassurance from your lover, you make a nurturing, caring, sensual, and romantic partner. You are very loyal in your relationships, and demand the same from your mate or partner. Infidelity threatens your sense of security and is, therefore, totally unacceptable.

Mars in Leo

Although Mars in Leo is noted for its fiery physical energy, you manage to shine in mental and practical arenas as well. At times, your leonine ego and deep-seated need for recognition make your emotional energy seem somewhat restrained, but the Martian lion projects an air of confidence, self-sufficiency, and vitality that causes other people to sit up and take notice. People with this placement are inherently ambitious and dramatic, and adore being center stage. Mars in Leo couples positive initiative with stability and determination, producing excellent leadership qualities. Proud, principled, and idealistic, you detest small-mindedness and disloyalty. In all things in life, you follow your heart. You make a warm and generous friend, lover, or relative, but you demand undivided devotion, understanding, and admiration in return.

The lion enjoys sex more than most, as long as heavy doses of love and romance are part of the package. As an affectionate, physically demonstrative lover, you take great pride in your sexual prowess and are easy to arouse. Your ideal mate radiates warmth and shows affection in a physical way. You're likely to be even more interested if a potential partner is rich, famous, powerful, or gorgeous, and thus able to reflect glory onto you. As much as it bolsters your ego to have several sexual partners, you tend to stay constant in love as long so your partner pays plenty of attention to you and remains devoted.

Mars in Virgo

An earthy and somewhat nervous sexuality characterizes those with this horoscope position. Although your physical needs are strong, you keep your emotions under strict control, making you are more than a little hesitant about letting yourself go. Because of the shy side to Virgo's nature, Mars, indicator of passion, often remains sublimated or un-awakened in this sign. However, you're a perfectionist and strive to be as good as possible at everything you do, including sex.

Typically, Virgo has a great sense of humor and appreciates wit in others, but not crudeness. You want a lover who can act with decorum in public, yet abandon his or her inhibitions in favor of an earthy lustiness in private. Although modest in public, your innate sensuality comes out of hiding in the bedroom. Your aim is to please—in bed and out—and you'll do as much or more than the other signs to ensure your partner's happiness.

Although insatiably curious about sex, you're not naturally wild or impulsive in your love life. You prefer carefully thinking things through. Martian Virgos love touching and being touched, but they're not interested in idle flirtations or one-night stands. You regard sex as a pleasurable and meaningful way to express genuine feelings of closeness and affection.

Mars in Libra

In Libra, Mars' energy is carefully controlled and decidedly more mental than physical. Those born under its auspices are diplomatic, charming, amiable, and convincing. With this Mars placement, normally assertive behavior is toned down, and passions are not allowed to rule thinking. Yet, despite your unemotional approach to most things, you can become quite upset if your perception of justice is not served. You easily get caught up in defending those who you believe are being treated inequitably.

Libra's sex drive is tempered by a reluctance to allow physical passion to rule intellect. More romantic than hot-blooded, you are searching for mental and emotional connections rather than physical passion. In relationships, you're agreeable, but not a pushover. Decisiveness is not the scales' strong point; but when you do decide what you want you know exactly what you need to do to get it. Libra's ideal lover is charming, well turned out, and classy. It certainly helps if he or she is also good-looking, intelligent, and sophisticated. You respond more readily to mental and verbal turn-ons than to physical ones and can be charmed by someone who is a creative smooth talker. Although you think you seek harmony and serenity, too much peace and quiet eventually bores you, and you enjoy shaking things up now and again.

Mars in Scorpio

In Scorpio, Mars displays powerful emotions and desires. Strong, self-reliant, efficient, and highly self-disciplined, your intensity of purpose permeates every task you undertake. Scorpios make loyal friends—and bitter enemies who never forget or forgive a betrayal. Slow to anger, you rarely lose control, but when your ire is raised you make it your business to get even, and you do so with frightening detachment.

Those with Mars in Scorpio become deeply attached, sometimes obsessively so, to whatever or whomever they fancy. Outwardly cool and composed, your powerful feelings smolder just below the surface and once you set a course, you pursue it with quiet determination and great thoroughness. In a love relationship, you can be notoriously jealous and possessive, vengeful if betrayed. But, when you feel secure and in control, you invest one hundred percent of yourself in the union. You expect no less in return.

In Scorpio, Mars projects a raw sexual energy that is sensed by others. Your sex drive is single-minded and passionate. No wimps need apply! The type of lover who attracts you has the kind of magnetic charisma that hints at smoldering sexuality and passion. Strong willed and possessive yourself, you look for the same qualities in a mate. You're often drawn to individuals who come off as powerful or dangerous. The person who seems mysterious or brooding, or appears to be hiding deep dark secrets, intrigues you.

Mars in Sagittarius

Mars in Sagittarius produces some of the highest levels of physical energy and enthusiasm in the zodiac. With your zest for adventure and love of change and travel, you have difficulty sitting still for very long. The hallmark of this position is a feeling of invincibility. You probably feel as if you were born under a lucky star. In actuality, you succeed in life because you do not consider failure an option.

Mars in this sign is spontaneous, optimistic, impatient, and argumentative. You approach sex as if it were a sport or game, something to be enjoyed, but not taken too seriously. You value your independence, are afraid of being tied down, and may decide to run off if things get too dull or boring. You want honesty, friendship, and fun in an intimate relationship. Sharing adventures or a philosophical discussion piques your interest, and a potential partner with a good sense of humor wins your affection. With this placement of Mars, you may fall in love with a friend, or have a fading romance turn into a lasting friendship.

Mars in Capricorn

In this sign, Mars' energy is more practical than enthusiastic. With fiery Mars in orderly Capricorn, you possess a subdued but determined approach to life. Goal-oriented and focused, you like staying on top of things, and aren't afraid of hard work. You tend to approach everything in life with a cool, level-headed manner. Whether expressing anger or sexuality, you believe that you must always maintain strict control over yourself and your feelings.

Your sex drive is powerful with a full appreciation of the sensual pleasures. However, despite your strong physical needs and desires, you typically choose self-discipline over self indulgence. Since Mars in Capricorn detests waste and fears disorderliness, you find "letting go" particularly difficult—in and out of the bedroom. But, beneath your restrained exterior you are sensitive, passionate, and very much in need of love and affection.

The potential lover who projects a hard-to-read inscrutability intrigues you. Your ideal mate is ambitious and socially acceptable, and you're drawn to money, status, and power. Basically practical and materialistic, those with Mars in Capricorn are often more concerned with financial security than sexiness or romance. Since you can be slow to show your own affections, you're comfortable with a suitor who takes time to commit. However, once you make up your mind, you play for keeps.

Mars in Aquarius

With Mars in Aquarius your emotional side may struggle because your energies are mainly focused on intellectual pursuits. Natives of this sign have an original view of the world, and it can be difficult to figure out what makes them tick. Since those with Mars in Aquarius enjoy confusing people, that's fine with them.

The freewheeling individualist with Mars in Aquarius will fight passionately for a cause or ideal, yet maintain a seemingly detached attitude when dealing with personal issues. The sexual side of love may not be all that important to you, but you're open-minded where sex is concerned and intrigued by novelty. Although the thought of intense involvement scares you, when you do decided to commit, it's usually for the long haul.

An interesting person who is a little eccentric intrigues and attracts you. Originality gets your attention, and unpredictability keeps you coming back for more. You're more likely to be aroused by intellectual curiosity than by sexual signals alone. People with Mars in Aquarius are often willing to experiment with different sexual styles; or try a taboo merely out of curiosity.

Mars in Pisces

In Pisces, Mars produces strong, intense, and unpredictable emotions. With assertiveness drowned in sympathy, those with Mars in Pisces are more receptive and sensitive than proactive. Much of your attitude towards life stems from your keen sensitivity to the feelings of others.

You clearly know what other people are feeling, and you're always ready to render assistance to those most in need of help. As a result, you're apt to express the energies of Mars in support of the defenseless or underprivileged.

Passive by nature, you go with the flow, typically letting life happen without trying to control its direction. You're romantic and sentimental, but your needs are emotional rather than physical. In many ways, your view of love is a fantasy with such high expectations that it is rarely achieved in real life. In intimate situations, you're not averse to playing games to get what you want, even though you don't always know exactly what that is.

Mild tempered and gentle, you move through life in a manner that can hardly be considered direct. Your ideal romantic partner is sensitive and imaginative. Mystery intrigues you, and the idea of a secret love affair can excite and entice you. Highly emotional types attract you, and you find sharing feelings seductive. Broken-hearted lovers, starving artists, and penniless poets tug on your heartstrings.

3

Sun/Mars Combinations: Your Sex Drive

THE COMBINATION OF THE SIGNS OF THE SUN AND MARS IN YOUR BIRTH CHART reveals your sexual strengths and insecurities, and the role sexuality plays in your life. The sexual characteristics of the signs differ greatly. The Sun in your horoscope symbolizes the primary archetypal energy of your essential self. Its sign in your birth chart denotes your individuality and personal approach to sexual experience. Mars, the embodiment of sexual energy, indicates your sex quotient—how you express (or repress) your sexuality, your attitude toward sex, the strength of your libido, and your sexual prowess.

By understanding the astrological dynamics of your own Sun/Mars combination, or that of your significant other or potential lover, you gain tremendous insight in to one of life's basic motivating forces: the sex drive.

Combinations of the Sun in Aries

Sun in Aries/Mars in Aries

It doesn't get much more fiery than this combination of the Sun and Mars. You're a force of nature, and as headstrong, rash, and impulsive about sex as you are about everything else. Since you enjoy the chase and relish the role of playful pursuer, you don't hesitate to seize the initiative. You're very clear about what turns you on, and what you like and dislike in bed. Matching wits with your lover in the bedroom is a potent aphrodisiac for you, and you quickly lose interest in a partner who is unable to keep up with you mentally—or physically. Yet in a fulfilling romantic union, you're capable of great loyalty and devotion.

Sun in Aries/Mars in Taurus

You have tremendous energy and great physical endurance, but can't be rushed or hurried. A slow, steady seduction ignites your powerful sex drive and earthy sensuality. In bed, you like touching and being touched, and initiating shared physical pleasures. However, your sensuality extends beyond the bedroom to other life areas. Your delight in the senses is particularly noticeable in the kitchen, where preparing a romantic meal or playfully feeding your partner, serves as erotic foreplay. Turned on by the beauty of nature, you enjoy making passionate love outdoors.

Sun in Aries/Mars in Gemini

Wildly social and endlessly curious, you want everything in life to be exciting and spontaneous, including sex, and your ideal mate shares your interest in exploring new sexual territory. Since your intellect is your most sensitive erogenous zone, lovemaking begins inside your head—

and your sensual body swiftly follows. You like discussing what you want to do—or have done to you—between the sheets. Although you enjoy sharing ideas with someone special, you value your independence so much that sustaining a long-term relationship can be difficult.

Sun in Aries/Mars in Cancer

Your erotic life is full of fire and crazy extremes. The contradictions in your sexual nature can cause you to veer erratically between aggression and passivity, periods of celibacy and times of lust. Despite Aries' craving for independence, before you can relax and let down your guard, you need to feel safe and comfortable with your lover. When you feel a strong connection between yourself and your bed partner, your sensuality is profound. Since you are a tactile person, exploring each other's bodies in a shared shower or luxurious bath can bring you closer in a playful way.

Sun in Aries/Mars in Leo

Inherently romantic and idealistic, you have a penchant for dramatizing and mythologizing every aspect of your life. Initially, you do everything possible to attract a perspective lover. Thanks to your sunny, fun-loving nature, this is rarely a problem. In the bedroom, you're an ardent, inventive, and attentive partner. Yet, even in your most intimate moments you can't resist the temptation to turn your bedroom activities into a stellar performance. While it doesn't take much to spark your fiery passion, you crave more than physical satisfaction; for you, a love union is a heart and soul experience.

Sun in Aries/Mars in Virgo

Considerably more self-controlled than other rams, you prefer not to rush into romantic entanglements. Even so, you possess a robust libido, and your passionate nature runs deep and true. As a result, your strongest impulse is to live and love by the demands of your heart. But sooner or later you must come to terms with the conflict caused by your yearning for both independence, and a committed relationship. A practical romantic, you need to know your partner well before feeling comfortable, but once you develop a sense of trust, you let go and become the amorous lover you were meant to be. Kind and generous in the bedroom, you enjoy exploring your bedmate's preferences along with your own.

Sun in Aries/Mars in Libra

Relationships are central to your life, and while you may admire those who choose a freewheeling lifestyle, you want the companionship of a fulfilling union more than your independence. While a part of you may yearn to break all the rules, you're mostly aroused by slow, sensual lovemaking. Happy to take the lead between the sheets, you also enjoy being seduced into sweet submission. You like being enticed into sex with kissing and touching designed to inflame your desire. Even so, an occasional erotic free-for-all satisfies your most primal urges.

Sun in Aries/Mars in Scorpio

Few can match the explosive passions and deeply felt sensuality of this ultrasexy combination. Your charisma and smoldering sexuality attract admirers by the droves; and you probably have the notches on your bedpost to prove it. Yet despite Mars in Scorpio's ranking among the most prodigious lovers in the zodiac, the physical side of lovemaking alone rarely satisfies you. You're seeking a transcendent experience, leading to a deeper union with your beloved. You're intensely emotional, yet less likely to show your true feelings than other Aries. Consequently, your anger simmers, eventually erupting in spite or biting sarcasm. Your ideal bedmate knows how to stand up to the unpredictable volatility that fuels your libido, without dampening your lusty enthusiasm.

Sun in Aries/Mars in Sagittarius

The happy-go-lucky, charming lovers born under this combination are looking for honesty, companionship, and fun in an intimate relationship. Your desire for independence and your adventurous nature make you likely to be drawn into spontaneous affairs that burn brightly, but are of short duration. Despite your fiery aggressiveness, you feel things very deeply. When you do become intensely involved with someone, you make a romantic, caring, and generous partner. Sex for you is something of a game, and you crave the same lack of restrictions in love that you seek in other areas. Versatility is your strong point—in bed and out—and you're willing to try anything at least once.

Sun in Aries/Mars in Capricorn

This combination makes you less impulsive than most other rams. Although strongly sexed and sensual, you're quite capable of controlling and directing your passions. Despite your reserve, you're a romantic idealist and a lot lustier than your outer demeanor suggests. You may have some difficulty expressing your emotions, but have no such problem with your libido. You relish the chase and, behind closed doors, make an exciting, ardent, and adventurous lover. You take your time choosing a life partner, but once you make the commitment you do everything possible to secure the relationship.

Sun in Aries/Mars in Aquarius

You may be a maverick and a nonconformist, but you're not a loner. In an intimate relationship, friendship and intellectual rapport are as important to you as love and romance. Still, there's nothing dull or boring about your approach to lovemaking, and sex with you is likely to be intense and frequent. Although lacking the patience for sultry seductive scenes, you don't hesitate to experiment with different sexual techniques. Between the sheets, you prefer slightly bawdy, rough-and-tumble romps, to overly sweet and sentimental lovemaking.

Sun in Aries/Mars in Pisces

Your restless Aries nature is continually at odds with Pisces' idealism; you yearn for an all-encompassing intimate relationship, but want the independence to follow your personal destiny. Because of this inner conflict, you may go through some pretty tempestuous romances before settling down with your one true love. You may be timid in some life areas, but the bedroom isn't one of them. The hot-blooded, uninhibited, passionate side of your nature practically guarantees a pleasurable time in bed and you enjoy experimenting with new ways of pleasing your partner. However, your sentimental side also enjoys quiet romantic evenings together just cuddling and kissing.

Combinations of the Sun in Taurus

Sun in Taurus/Mars in Aries

Your approach to love combines fiery Mars in Aries' urgent intensity with the earthy sensuality of your Sun in Taurus. What you want most from an intimate union is affection, emotional security, and lots of great sex, which to you means an ardent, exciting, but basically uncomplicated physical relationship. You enjoy making love, and your physical prowess enhances the sexual experience. You also like a good helping of romance in your bedroom activities, but only to a point. Not the most patient of Taurus lovers, once aroused, you want action, not talk.

Sun in Taurus/Mars in Taurus

In an intimate union, you are sensual, passionate, caring, and generous. Good sex ranks high on your list of life's priorities, and your approach to lovemaking is tactile and erotic. Physical intimacy energizes your body and nourishes your inner being. Although you enjoy experimenting with a variety of sexual positions and techniques, you find the warmth of close contact and shared affection most satisfying. Most of the time, you're relaxed and full of fun, but can sometimes be jealous and demanding.

Sun in Taurus/Mars in Gemini

As a romantic partner, you're affectionate, sensual, and exciting. A delightfully verbal and physical lover, you have a knack for turning subtle innuendo and clever quips into masterful tools of seduction. Spicy sexual banter allows you to share whatever you're thinking and feeling with your partner. Although you relish physical pleasure, there is also a mental component to your sexuality that longs to establish intellectual rapport. You enjoy the stability of a serious relationship, but too much togetherness may make you decidedly uncomfortable.

Sun in Taurus/Mars in Cancer

To be truly happy, you need a stable home life and the closeness of a committed, long-term relationship. Even so, it usually takes more than just affection and devotion to hold your interest. What you really crave is the electric intensity of sexual chemistry and strong physical passion. You may be reserved in public, but once you close the bedroom door you make love with abandon. A powerhouse of sexual vitality, you rely on a combination of patience and physical stamina to build slowly to a peak of ecstasy.

Sun in Taurus/Mars in Leo

Sensual and strongly sexed, your deep-seated need for love and affection makes you an ardent and passionate lover. Physical intimacy and demonstrations of love make you feel totally alive. Taurus's earthy sensuality is imbued with Leo's flair for the dramatic, and you're not above strutting your stuff in the bedroom. A generous, considerate bedmate, you're concerned with pleasing your partner, and happy to cater to his or her wishes as long as you receive the same type of treatment in return. Tactile by nature, you regard lovemaking as a carnival of the senses during which you enjoy each and every ride.

Sun in Taurus/Mars in Virgo

For you, communication and chemistry are prerequisites to any close relationship. Wild fantasy and theatrics in the bedroom are not your style. You crave the transcendent and uncomplicated lovemaking of an enduring union that serves as an anchor for an ordered life. You respond readily to the lover who arouses your senses with passionate kisses and intimate caresses. Although not bold enough to suggest erotic innovation yourself, you welcome a more adventurous bed partner. Thrilled by the idea of forbidden fruit, you can develop a taste for bawdy sexual antics, as long as they're not too outrageous.

Sun in Taurus/Mars in Libra

Despite your practical, down-to-earth nature, you crave both passion and romance in the bedroom. For you, one of the best things about an intimate relationship is the shared experience of exploring your physical senses through sexual contact. When you find Mr. or Ms. Right, you're capable of remaining loyal and committed to the end. However, because of your romantic idealism, problems may arise regarding the way a close union should function.

Sun in Taurus/Mars in Scorpio

You are gifted with a lush sensuality that attracts potential suitors to you, but the foolhardy lover who mistakes your smoldering sexual magnetism for easy prey soon learns not to trifle with your affections. Your quiet reserve masks a determined will and, when you're the one smitten, your caution quickly gives way to seduction. However, while the joy of sensate pleasure may draw you in, it takes a meaningful connection to hold your interest.

Sun in Taurus/Mars in Sagittarius

Taurus wants the emotional security sought by all bulls, but the Martian archer in you yearns for independence. However, when you close your bedroom door, you leave everything disagreeable or unpleasant on the other side. Naturally tactile, you enjoy stroking and touching your partner, and being similarly caressed in return. Yet, for you, lusty sensuality is only part of the package. The lover who shows how much he or she truly cares is the one who gets your juices flowing.

Sun in Taurus/Mars in Capricorn

You're as warm-blooded and affectionate as other Taurus natives, but less comfortable about letting your deepest feelings show. Simmering just beneath your seemingly imperturbable exterior is a warm sensuality that emerges behind closed doors. When you feel safe and secure in a loving union, you delight in physical love. You possess a powerful sex drive and are skilled at satisfying your bedmate's desires. Moreover, you like to take your time between the sheets and pride yourself on your ability to control and direct your passion.

Sun in Taurus/Mars in Aquarius

Your affable, gregarious personality covers a detached, somewhat impersonal inner core that allows you to keep your cool under emotional pressure. Earthy, sensual, and innovative, you like experimenting with various positions during lovemaking. You bring the joy of discovery to everything you do, and appreciate a bed partner who shares your uninhibited approach to sexuality. A playful lover, you find it fun to be unconventional in the bedroom, yet also enjoy making love in comfortable luxurious surroundings. You make a loyal and devoted life partner—once you decide to commit—but until then you're perfectly capable of enjoying a romantic alliance free of fetters.

Sun in Taurus/Mars in Pisces

One part of you is dreamy and romantic, the other sensible and down to earth. Your sensual nature appreciates the physical side of love, while your idealism engages the spiritual side. When you make a genuine connection you share all of yourself with your beloved, and know how to elevate lovemaking to an art form. At times you can be possessive, demanding, or clingy, but more often you're generous, considerate, and indulgent of your partner's wishes. You adore long, lazy hours of loving, during which you and your partner take the time to explore each other's bodies from head to toe.

Combinations of the Sun in Gemini

Sun in Gemini/Mars in Aries

Passionate and idealistic, you fall in and out of love rather easily. It takes both chemistry and intellectual rapport to capture your heart. Unless there's depth to your love connection, you begin to lose interest. Being friends with your lover is really important to you, and you're considerably more ardent than most Geminis. You view lovemaking as a fun-filled game, and manage to avoid bedroom boredom by employing a broad range of sexual techniques.

Sun in Gemini/Mars in Taurus

Your Mars in Taurus combination makes you more touchy feely than other twins—and more likely to enjoy foreplay that includes protracted periods of kissing and stroking. A sophisticated lover, you know how to tantalize your mate with an elegant courtship that builds slowly toward a peak of pleasure. In the bedroom, you like to feel that you're the center of your lover's world, and delight in knowing that he or she is turned on by you. Both sensuous and curious, you're eager to explore new ways to prolong and heighten the shared ecstasy.

Sun in Gemini/Mars in Gemini

This double dose of Gemini makes you restless and unpredictable in close relationships. At times, you're so mistrustful of your own emotions that you may try to rationalize them out of existence. In order to hold your love and attention, your significant other must find a way to engage your intellect along with your emotions. Your brain is your most prominent sex organ, and you enjoy sharing thoughts and ideas with your lover—along with your body. Clever verbal foreplay is your forte, and your silver-tongued seduction technique is witty and amusing. For you, sex is mainly fun and games, and not to be taken too seriously.

Sun in Gemini/Mars in Cancer

With your birth Mars in sentimental Cancer, you believe that love makes the world go 'round, and have some rather old-fashioned notions of what an intimate union should be. Even so, your playful approach in the bedroom can cause your lover to forget that you actually take love-making very seriously. When you feel comfortable and secure, there's no limit to what you will do to keep your partner happy. While you may appear reserved in public, behind closed doors you're ardent and sensual and want a lover who knows how to unleash your simmering passions.

Sun in Gemini/Mars in Leo

Yours is a romantic nature, and intimate relationships mean a great deal to you. Your approach to sexuality is both emotional and cerebral—just the thought of making love serves as a major turn-on. An inventive bed partner, you infuse a spirit of discovery and a sense of fun into your lovemaking. You enjoy pillow talk, sharing erotic fantasies, and exchanging spicy verbal banter beneath the covers. Together with your ideal lover, you kindle the sparks until they turn into a raging fire.

Sun in Gemini/Mars in Virgo

In a loving union, you're sexy and romantic but not starry eyed. Although a caring and affectionate lover, you're unlikely to forgo compatibility and communication in favor of moonlight and roses. Talking about ideas and sharing information makes you feel closer to your significant other—mentally and physically. Your libido is sparked by mental images of what you plan to do, and you find verbal stimulation as exciting as physical foreplay. While you may come off as shy, behind closed doors—and with the right bed partner—you're liable to try anything.

Sun in Gemini/Mars in Libra

You like being connected to another person and feel incomplete without a close relationship. Your fantasy of a loving union does not always include lots of sex. For you, a rousing debate or spirited conversation can be as exciting as a passionate sexual encounter. You're not comfortable with emotional intimacy, yet on a physical level you can be totally uninhibited. An adventurous lover, your aim is to please and be pleased. If you don't know what your partner likes in bed, you ask.

Sun in Gemini/Mars in Scorpio

Mars in Scorpio adds a note of paradox to your Sun in Gemini that may puzzle even those closest to you. The twins' open, easygoing nature is often in conflict with the suspicious scorpion's inherent secrecy, and you're often torn between the contradictory messages you receive from your head and your heart. A chameleon in the bedroom as elsewhere, you're an odd combination of passion and intellect. Sometimes you come off as playful and lighthearted, yet other nights nothing seems to matter except your intense sexuality and desire for physical gratification. Either way, no partner of yours is ever bored in bed.

Sun in Gemini/Mars in Sagittarius

Totally convinced that variety is the spice of life, you're constantly on the lookout for new experiences and challenges. A born hunter, you approach each perspective lover with the same passion that you bring to all your interests and having sex is one of your favorite things. In fact, it's right up there with rousing debates, traveling, and meeting new people. In a romantic union, you're generous and eager for love, but tend to be something of a romantic gypsy, and if the closeness becomes cloying, you may suddenly take off in search of a less restrictive relationship.

Sun in Gemini/Mars in Capricorn

You have a friendly, outgoing manner and a way with words that attracts many interesting acquaintances. Where romance is concerned, you tend to analyze everything about a potential partner before even considering an alliance. In public, you shy away from displays of affection, but the privacy of the bedroom brings out your steamy sensuality. You yearn for a physical relationship that takes you and your lover to the heights of passion. However, for this to happen, your mind must be stimulated along with your body.

Sun in Gemini/Mars in Aquarius

The charming, quick-witted individuals born under this combination are sociable and easygoing, but wary of any situation that makes you feel emotionally vulnerable. As an innovative lover and inventive bedmate, you're always open to novel ideas for sexual experimentation. Once you get going between the sheets, you're a skillful, considerate lover intent on heightening the pleasure of both partners. However, it takes more than sex to hold your attention. If your lover is unable to have an intelligent conversation, you swiftly lose interest. When involved in a committed union, you're loyal as long as your beloved respects your need for personal space.

Sun in Gemini/Mars in Pisces

You possess an elusive, ethereal quality that sets you apart from others with the Sun in Gemini. Even in the bedroom, you are something of an enigma. On one hand, you're a sensitive, alluring lover capable of extraordinary tenderness. On the other, your sexual approach is so rational that it may seem calculated. Either way you thrive in an atmosphere of fun and creativity and enjoy trying new exotic things in bed as long as they're not crude or vulgar. To a great extent, the intensity of your sex drive depends on your vibrant imagination. A master storyteller, you're turned on by a lover with a fantasy life equal to your own. When your intellect is stimulated by erotic sexual banter with your mate, your physical body quickly follows suit.

Combinations of the Sun in Cancer

Sun in Cancer/Mars in Aries

Despite your desire for intimacy, you're basically moody and shift back and forth between your need for security and yearning for personal freedom. As a result, you're nurturing, generous, and loyal in a close relationship, but can also be temperamental, demanding, and possessive. In bed, you know how to combine tenderness and consideration with intense passion and erotic excitement. Trying new things excites you and keeps your lovemaking fresh and interesting. If you sense love and approval from your lover, you won't hesitate to venture into previously untried sexual territory.

Sun in Cancer/Mars in Taurus

Sensitive and deeply emotional, you respond intuitively to other people's needs and desires. You're more likely to be moved by another person's actions than by his or her words and long for a calm, stable home life and the closeness of a committed union. A passionate lover, you revel in the sensual pleasures of lovemaking. You take great joy in lavishing love and affection on your partner, and expect the same consideration in return. Emotional bonding is as important to you as physical union, and you want to know that you and your partner are on the same page as far as your relationship is concerned.

Sun in Cancer/Mars in Gemini

While more relaxed than other crabs, you're still subject to the frequent mood swings typical of Cancers. Sometimes it is difficult for you to reconcile the lighthearted, flirtatious side of your nature with your deep emotional need for the security of a permanent love union. Communication is extremely important to you in an intimate alliance. Unlike many members of your Sun sign, you enjoy expressing your lusty desires verbally, with sexy erotic banter. You get off on talking about your own thoughts and feelings and, with your seductive aura and sensitivity to your partner's moods and desires, you can be absolutely irresistible in the bedroom.

Sun in Cancer/Mars in Cancer

Emotional vulnerability is a major trait with this natal Sun/Mars combination, and you're not about to put your heart on the line unless you are sure that your feelings are reciprocated. You like to establish strong connections to your partner before embarking on a physical relationship. You're no prude, but casual sex just doesn't do it for you. Once involved, you want lots of romance and sexual affection. You shine in unhurried moments of languid lovemaking, and hugging, kissing, touching, and other preliminaries are vitally important.

Sun in Cancer/Mars in Leo

There is a theatrical side to your nature that craves drama and adventure in an intimate union, but high ideals dictate your actions, even in the bedroom, and casual affairs hold little temptation for you. You regard a sexual relationship as a genuine partnership, especially if you're acknowledged as senior partner. Although you can't help but assume the dominant role, your mate's happiness and gratification is always foremost in your mind. A delightfully romantic, imaginative lover, you'll go to great pains to create a sumptuous, relaxing setting for love and enjoy basking in the erotic pleasures of slow, sensual lovemaking in the elegant comfort of beautiful, luxurious surroundings.

Sun in Cancer/Mars in Virgo

People born under this Sun/Mars combination are romantic idealists who don't give their hearts away easily and the intensity of your sexuality is closely connected to the depth of your feelings. You fear rejection and can be jealous and possessive of your beloved. Even so, in a committed relationship you make a loyal, caring, and considerate partner. Passionate on one hand and tender on the other, you love to kiss, cuddle, and just hang out with your lover.

Sun in Cancer/Mars in Libra

You're a romantic idealist, and likely to hold off making a serious commitment until you're sure that you've found Mr. or Ms. Right. Once involved, you make a wonderfully nurturing, refined, thoughtful, and protective lover. In the bedroom, your sensual desires are heightened by feelings of a strong intuitive connection to your partner. Although your lovemaking propensities lean toward the traditional, you're willing to put your own inclinations aside in order to please your bedmate. When your lover is happy, you're happy too.

Sun in Cancer/Mars in Scorpio

You make an exceedingly loyal and caring mate or partner, but are fearful of exposing your vulnerability. Even so, when you find the person you want you'll stop at nothing to turn your dream into a reality. Despite your jealousy, you're sensual, romantic, and passionate, and your emotional and physical intensity make for endlessly thrilling bedroom encounters. Stamina is your forte, and your bedmate looks forward to adventurous nights—and days—of innovative and inventive sexual pleasures engendered by your lusty libido. Experimenting with exotic techniques keeps your sex life fresh and exciting.

Sun in Cancer/Mars in Sagittarius

This combination often manifests as a deep-seated inner conflict; Sagittarius wants travel, excitement, and adventure, but Cancer craves roots and the safety of a secure home life. Despite your seemingly traditional attitude toward sexuality, you long to be swept away on a wave of passionate, ecstatic lovemaking. Spontaneity and fun turn you on as readily as the most ardent foreplay. Your ideal bedmate understands your paradoxical nature, and appeases your thrill-seeking side by lovingly luring you into uncharted sexual territory within a committed relationship. The intuitive lover whose lack of inhibitions behind closed doors matches your own, knows what to do to satisfy your strong, secret cravings.

Sun in Cancer/Mars in Capricorn

Those with this combination believe that sex should be part of a lifestyle that includes all the elements of a committed relationship. Although commonly a workaholic, your well-defined domestic side craves the comfort and security of home and family. At times your sexual nature seems out of balance with the rest of your life, and prone to contradictions and inconsistencies. However, once you find the love and acceptance you seek, you make a passionate, responsive lover, as well as a caring, dependable life partner.

Sun in Cancer/Mars in Aquarius

At times your emotions are so contradictory that you don't even know what you truly want. Home- and family-oriented, you often feel conflicted between your desire for commitment, and your yearning for freedom and independence. Ultimately, your ideal relationship is well rounded, and appeals to both the emotional and intellectual sides of your nature. Feelings of closeness to your mate inflame your desires and increase your appetite for physical intimacy. An innovative lover, you enjoy spontaneity and inventiveness in the bedroom as much as sensuality and romance. Your ability to combine subtle seduction with a bit of fun and games keeps your lovemaking fresh and exciting.

Sun in Cancer/Mars in Pisces

With both the Sun and Mars in Water signs, you're motivated by your emotions, instead of your intellect or body. For you, lovemaking is more than a mere physical act, but a total intimacy involving your body, mind, and soul. Mutual give and take is important to you—in the bedroom and elsewhere. Once involved, you soak up your significant other's feelings and desires like a psychic sponge; sometimes you have a hard time separating what you're feeling from what you're picking up from your companion.

Combinations of the Sun in Leo

Sun in Leo/Mars in Aries

This combination produces fiery, passionate lovers who are rarely shy about going after what they want. You adore the spotlight and tend to view your activities—both in and out of the bedroom—as command performances. While it doesn't take much to rouse your lusty sexual appetite, true love is your best aphrodisiac. Your intense romantic idealism causes you to view your love relationship as sacred and larger than life. Moreover, you crave more than mere physical satisfaction in bed; your aim is to turn your union into a transcendent experience.

Sun in Leo/Mars in Taurus

A genuine romantic, you tend to view courtship as an ongoing ritual, and can be quite lavish in expressing your feelings. Your sexual approach is a combination of solar Leo's fiery passion with Mars in Taurus's languid sensuality. More than willing to pamper and indulge your partner, you expect to be catered to and admired in return. You view lovemaking as a carnival of the senses, and your bedroom as an intimate stage for erotic enjoyment. When you're in the mood for love, you pursue the object of your affection with leonine intensity. If a relationship turns sour you're devastated, but aren't likely to remain alone for long.

Sun in Leo/Mars in Gemini

Less dramatic than other Leos, you have a laid-back approach to love and sexuality. Your fun and games tactics in the bedroom practically guarantee you and your partner a good time between the sheets. Essentially more cerebral than emotional, you have a way with words that rarely fails to arouse your bed partner. However, once your strong sex drive takes over, witty sexual banter swiftly gives way to passionate lovemaking. The ability to please as well as be pleased is important to you, and you pride yourself on remembering the little details that make your partner feel truly loved.

Sun in Leo/Mars in Cancer

Loving and protective by nature, you're warm, passionate, and exceedingly generous, but can also be possessive and demanding. You require a good deal of emotional pampering, and are at your best in a love union where you get the attention and devotion you crave. Inherently sexy and passionate, you're driven by a lusty libido and strong sense of the dramatic. Your exceptional intuition helps you pick up on your partner's feelings and anticipate his or her desires—in and out of bed. This ability to provide what the other person wants makes you virtually irresistible as a lover.

Sun in Leo/Mars in Leo

This double dose of Fire energy shows that you're a force to be reckoned with. Typically, the lion is an extrovert, but even the shyest of the great cats craves the approbation and applause of an audience. A genuine romantic, you dramatize and mythologize every aspect of your life. Your physical passions and sexual prowess are equal to those of the most ardent Aries or Scorpio, but your leonine ego is surprisingly fragile and requires frequent encouragement and reassurance. Since flattery is Leo's ultimate aphrodisiac, nothing turns you on faster than the approval of a loving bedmate.

Sun in Leo/Mars in Virgo

You're caring and loyal, but romantic idealism and a desire for perfection can undermine your relationships. You require a great deal of attention and pampering, and when you get it you're much less inclined to find fault with your mate. In the privacy of the bedroom, you're a sensual, passionate lover who demonstrates affection through deeds as well as words. You possess a vivid imagination and acting out erotic fantasies appeals to your sense of the theatrical. Sexy attire turns you on and, with a partner you trust, you enjoy simulating fanciful scenes of torrid seduction.

Sun in Leo/Mars in Libra

Everything that is beautiful, harmonious, and tasteful appeals to you, but you expect so much from an intimate union that the reality rarely lives up to your mental image. When you find your true love, you make a generous, caring, and enthusiastic life partner, but also an extremely demanding one. In bed, you thrive in the company of a partner who showers you with attention and approval. Despite your strong sexual appetite, your ultimate aim is to take lovemaking to a higher, more esoteric level than mere physical gratification.

Sun in Leo/Mars in Scorpio

Your exuberant surface personality conceals a very un-Leo-like inner nature that is secretive and mysterious. In love and romance, you are intensely passionate, extremely complex, and determined to have things your own way. A generous lover, you're eager to please and usually willing to try new things in the bedroom; you'll use everything in your bag of tricks to arouse your partner and build the sexual excitement to an ecstatic finale. A master of nonverbal communication, you prefer expressing your innermost feelings through sensual contact. Although you enjoy showy gestures, underneath the theatricality you're genuinely caring and considerate.

Sun in Leo/Mars in Sagittarius

You fall in love easily, but if things get too heavy, you may get antsy and think about moving on. When you do settle down, your ideal partner is one who shares your love of travel, excitement, and adventure. Sensuality is your weakness, and you enjoy being stroked, fondled, and fussed over. You particularly like it when your bed partner makes a special effort to seduce you with erotic toys, sexy apparel, and provocative language.

Sun in Leo/Mars in Capricorn

Although this combination can be demanding, when you feel safe and secure in an intimate union you're caring, protective, generous, and loyal. Behind closed doors, you make a fiery, dramatic bedmate with an exceedingly physical approach to lovemaking. A powerhouse of sexual energy, you like being the one in control of your sexual encounters. Casual bedroom dalliances don't appeal to you. You prefer saving your passionate ardor for a grand affair of the heart. In the right situation, with the right person, you dazzle your bed partner with a combination of aggressive moves and lingering sensual caresses.

Sun in Leo/Mars in Aquarius

Love may make your world go around, but you're independent enough not to allow it to rule your life. You make a generous, thoughtful, exciting lover for as long as the relationship is not overly confining. Although solitude holds little appeal for you, not even your dearest love can get away with telling you what to do. You want an intimate union where love and friendship coexist, and quickly lose interest in romance that lacks a mental connection. In the bedroom, your curious mind and yearning for discovery prompt you to try new things and venture into previously unexplored sexual territory.

Sun in Leo/Mars in Pisces

Your personality is a complex mixture of confidence and uncertainty. Although your inner lion craves the spotlight, the fish prefers operating behind the scenes. This chameleon-like aspect of your nature provides endless fascination in the bedroom. You're quite capable of enchanting your lover with subtle seductive moves one night, then dazzling him or her with sizzling intensity and wild abandon the next. You're so psychic that you pick up your partner's thoughts, and your ability to intuit your mate's desires makes it easy for you to gratify them.

Combinations of the Sun in Virgo

Sun in Virgo/Mars in Aries

With this combo in your birth chart you may find yourself torn between opposing influences. While the more precipitous Aries prompts you to rush headlong into an intimate relationship, cautious Virgo reminds you to think twice. Physically passionate, you tend to blow hot and cold emotionally. Even so, you are considerably more romantic then you care to admit. When you find security and contentment in a love union, you make a loving, caring, and affectionate partner. A totally different person in private than in public, behind closed doors you drop your reserve and give full rein to your sexuality.

Sun in Virgo/Mars in Taurus

While some romantic partners may be more exciting, few are as dependable or trustworthy. Although otherwise practical and sensible, in the bedroom your old-fashioned romanticism, earthy sensuality, and consideration for your partner make you an excellent lover. You enjoy touching and being touched, and your heightened sensory perception enhances the pleasure you share with your partner. It doesn't take a lot of frills to entice you, but you do appreciate the beauty of an elegantly appointed room. A clean, pleasant atmosphere with fresh flowers, scented candles, and soft music playing in the background puts you in the mood for love.

Sun in Virgo/Mars in Gemini

Although you adore partying and flirting, you require the stability of a long-term love union. While your approach to love and sex may come off as emotionally cool and lighthearted, you have a serious appreciation for the physical joys of lovemaking. A skilled lover, you're fascinated with the mechanics and techniques of sexuality. Nevertheless, your approach to the erotic pleasures of the body is earthy, direct, and decidedly unpretentious. Since you're motivated as much by curiosity as by desire, change and variety spice up your love life and keep you interested—in bed and out.

Sun in Virgo/Mars in Cancer

With this combination, you need a significant other who makes you feel cherished and appreciated. At times you exude an aura of cool detachment, and sexually you can be elusive, mysterious, and enigmatic. Although you tend to keep your feelings under control in public, in private you're warm and loving. Even so, it's unlikely that a purely sexual relationship will satisfy you. You're looking for something much deeper in a partnership. With the right bed partner, the complex layers of your earthy sensuality begin to unfold and—behind closed doors—your passionate side surfaces. A curious mate interested in experimentation between the sheets brings out the carnality in your nature.

Sun in Virgo/Mars in Leo

You're deeply passionate and exude a type of smoldering sexuality that potential suitors find exceedingly appealing. In a close relationship, romance truly matters, but so does intellectual rapport. Your high ideals extend to the bedroom, and casual affairs hold little temptation for you. You possess deep levels of sexual desire that need to be drawn out slowly over time. Your ideal lover knows how to be thrilling and entertaining, without overstepping the bounds of good taste.

Sun in Virgo/Mars in Virgo

Not one to leap into a romantic union with reckless abandon, you get to know a potential lover first, preferably through sharing interests outside the boudoir. A confirmed workaholic, you may appear less interested in sex and romance than you actually are. However, once you stop overanalyzing every move you make—and start heeding the promptings of your feelings and emotions—you are an exceptionally passionate, considerate partner. In the privacy of the bedroom, the sensual side of your nature comes to the forefront. You have plenty of sexual curiosity, and are always seeking new ways to excite and pleasure your mate.

Sun in Virgo/Mars in Libra

Your high expectations where love is concerned can make it difficult for you to reach a concrete decision about the future of a romantic relationship. However, once you decide, you hang in for the long term. Physical intimacy isn't a problem for you, because you regard sex as the one of the purest forms of communication. More than anything, you want a harmonious, satisfying love life—for both you and your partner. Since you view sex as a two-way street, you expect to receive the same kind of consideration that you show your bedmate.

Sun in Virgo/Mars in Scorpio

This merger of solar Virgo's analytical intellect with the Martian scorpion's powerful emotions produces a nature that is cool and reserved on the outside with a passionate intensity smoldering beneath the surface. Your ability to analyze things before taking action makes you a methodical, creative, and innovative lover. You think of a game plan and then put it into motion in the bedroom—with satisfying results. In creating the perfect setting for lovemaking, you pay scrupulous attention to the smallest details. You do everything possible to please your lover, but expect similar treatment in return.

Sun in Virgo/Mars in Sagittarius

Virgo makes you cautious and sensible, but the fiery archer within clamors for adventure and excitement. In a committed relationship, you require more freedom and independence than most other virgins, but sharing your ideas and insights makes you feel closer to your partner. Sexually, you're tender and ardent, and like to spoil your lover. Your ideal bed partner also understands *your* need to be catered to and pampered. A slow artful seduction appeals to your refined sensibilities and erotic foreplay turns you on, setting the stage for deeper, more meaningful lovemaking.

Sun in Virgo/Mars in Capricorn

Although you appear composed on the surface, you often feel insecure and emotionally vulnerable. You have difficulty expressing yourself, and your true emotions are not likely to be revealed until you get to know your partner well. Nevertheless, your sex drive is strong and, when you let yourself go, you're a sexy, sensuous lover. In the privacy of the bedroom, you drop your reserved demeanor and reveal your inherent passion. The patient bedmate who draws out your hidden desires is well rewarded. An erotic massage at the hands of your lover reconnects you with your lusty libido.

Sun in Virgo/Mars in Aquarius

In close relationships, you rarely act the way others expect, and may appear to be disinterested in intimacy and commitment. However, once involved, you make a loyal, devoted partner. For you, sexual arousal begins in the mind, and when your intellect is engaged, your body swiftly follows. The wise lover knows how to loosen you up with provocative language and witty erotic banter. Since you enjoy sexual experimentation, you make an innovative and inventive bed partner. Once you understand what pleases your partner in bed, you're usually more than willing to comply.

Sun in Virgo/Mars in Pisces

Sensual, sensitive, and concerned, you're a very easy person to love. Making your partner feel cherished and appreciated is your special talent, in bed and out. For you, physical love is a tender expression of deeper feelings; a complete and total mingling of body, mind, and soul. You want a partner who is everything to you: lover, friend, spiritual companion, and creative equal. When you find true love, you willingly sacrifice all for your partner. In return, you expect a sexual experience that is perfect, an effortless meshing of physical pleasure, emotional fulfillment, and intellectual understanding.

Combinations of the Sun in Libra

Sun in Libra/Mars in Aries

Aggressive one moment and laid-back the next, you move unexpectedly between overt passion and subtle seduction. The ardent side of your nature longs to be swept away in an erotic free-for-all, but you enjoy being wooed and won in an old-fashioned romantic courtship. Still, your refined manner never quite overcomes the animal lustiness lurking beneath the surface; the part of you that longs to break all the rules responds readily to the innovative, uninhibited lover who entices you with provocative suggestions.

Sun in Libra/Mars in Taurus

The "urge to merge" is the main motivation for people with this combination. You're among the most sensual and sexually active members of your Sun sign, and possess a sixth sense regarding your partner's needs and desires. Since you crave beauty and order in your life, a harmonious environment puts you in the mood for love. You revel in the carnival of the senses created by sultry nightwear, luxurious bed linens, fresh flowers, scented candles, and soft music playing in the background.

Sun in Libra/Mars in Gemini

Although you long for a permanent relationship, you can be fickle in your attachments; one part of you wants commitment, another freedom. Intellectual companionship is as vital to you as romance, and a spirited discussion is as stimulating as a passionate sexual encounter. A delightful mixture of fun-filled companion and romantic partner, you love deeply without taking things all that seriously. While willing to do whatever it takes to make your mate happy, you won't surrender your soul in the process. In the bedroom, your quick wit and fluency with language are your most powerful means of seduction.

Sun in Libra/Mars in Cancer

Outwardly you may act as if romance is all fun and games, but in matters of the heart you play for keeps. You have a strongly sensual nature, yet in order to be truly satisfied you need a partner you really care about and who cares about you. No one expects more from a lover than you do. You regard love as the highest ideal possible, and sex exalts your being at every level. In the bedroom, you're something of a perfectionist and you refuse to put up with halfway measures. Your lovemaking style is as slow and intense as it is passionate and transformative.

Sun in Libra/Mars in Leo

You like being the star of your own drama, especially in the bedroom. Once involved with someone, you make a generous, caring, and enthusiastic romantic partner, but you crave admiration and approval almost as much as love and affection. Since you view sex as an art, you require a certain amount of sophistication and good taste in a lover. Your delicate sensibilities are easily offended by boorish behavior between the sheets. A harmonious atmosphere with luxurious bedding and scented candles makes you feel sensuous and sexy.

Sun in Libra/Mars in Virgo

Naturally peace loving and amenable, you go out of your way to avoid discord or disagreement, and you refuse to settle for less than perfection in a partner. As a result, it may take you a while to make a firm commitment, but once you do, you expect the relationship to last forever. In the bedroom you're prepared to invest a great deal of energy in creating a satisfying intimate union. A sensual, patient lover, you wait for the perfect time to make your move, and a slow, artful, sexy seduction is more your style than aggressive lovemaking.

Sun in Libra/Mars in Libra

Your genial disposition and willingness to compromise make you particularly easy to get along with. You thrive on the affection and attention of your mate, and are easily influenced by his or her opinions and ideas. Your refined nature wants lovemaking to be serene and beautiful, and romance is as important to you as passion. You're especially turned on by thoughtful, romantic gifts such as wine, candy, or a bunch of flowers. Naturally thoughtful and considerate, you tend to put your bed partner's happiness and satisfaction ahead of your own, but you expect the same thoughtfulness and consideration in return.

Sun in Libra/Mars in Scorpio

The glamorous aura you project can be utterly captivating, but you're discriminating when it comes to romantic involvement. You're looking for a genuine soul mate, and refuse to settle for less. In the bedroom, you're an irresistible combination of red-hot passion and old-fashioned romance. Your amorous nature thrives on the rituals of traditional courtship—sultry nightwear, silky sheets, and soft lighting. Then, with the stage set, you're ready to indulge in the erotic pleasures that love has to offer.

Sun in Libra/Mars in Sagittarius

A true romantic, you yearn for love and companionship. Pleasing your mate is important to you and you'll do almost anything to gratify his or her bedroom desires. You don't expect to be swept away by wild passion, but do appreciate a bedmate skilled in the ways of love. Dull or routine turns you off; you prefer a creative lover who knows how to keep you guessing. Spontaneous romantic gestures add sparkle to your bedroom activities and, whether watching or participating, a sultry, sensual striptease energizes your libido and gets your sexual juices flowing.

Sun in Libra/Mars in Capricorn

Outwardly you appear as easygoing as other Librans, yet a fierce determination to succeed is lurking just beneath the surface. You need to be with someone with a strong sense of purpose who shares your goals. In the bedroom, you're a study in contrasts; at times sentimental and affectionate, at others lusty and passionate. Your sexual feelings may run hot and cold, but when they're hot they sizzle. Endurance is your forte, and your appetite for sensual pleasures increases over time. The longer you and your lover are together, the more uninhibited you are in his or her embrace. During your wilder moments, you pull out all the stops and give full reign to your sexual needs and desires.

Sun in Libra/Mars in Aquarius

For the most part, you favor romantic rituals of love and courtship over the unbridled passion of earthy sexual encounters. A generous lover, you won't hesitate to put your own needs on hold in order to accommodate those of your partner. Between the sheets, you're erotically creative without ever being crude or vulgar. Since your physical responses are directly connected to your intellect, verbal communication is your forte—and you use it to your best advantage. Telling your lover what you want to do in the bedroom serves as a major turn-on, and makes your bedroom high jinks that much hotter.

Sun in Libra/Mars in Pisces

You hold some unrealistic ideas about love and relationships that can cause you great pain if things don't go as expected. Instead of dealing with disappointment head on, your inclination is to don rose-colored glasses and tell yourself everything is okay, even when it isn't. Since it's more natural for you to give than receive, nothing makes you happier than the opportunity to please your lover. But you shouldn't forget that turnabout is fair play, and you're equally entitled to pleasure. Luckily, you possess the ability to make your desires known with little more than a subtle hint or provocative glance.

Combinations of the Sun in Scorpio

Sun in Scorpio/Mars in Aries

This combination is one of the sexiest in the zodiac. You project an aura of mystery that others find intriguing, and few can resist your magnetic personality and smoldering sexuality. Although hard to live with, you're fiercely loyal to those you love. In an intimate union, you are loving and passionate, but also demanding and not easily pleased. Your ardent intensity and all-or-nothing approach in the bedroom takes your partner's breath away. The passionate, extremely physical lovemaking you favor requires an ardent bedmate with unflagging stamina equal to your own.

Sun in Scorpio/Mars in Taurus

Sexy and affectionate, you're made for grand passion and, when truly smitten, your normally cautious approach gives way to open seduction. You know exactly what to do to ignite the fires of love, and your ardor and intensity have a mesmerizing effect on all who fall under your spell. Casual affairs don't turn you on, because you long to transcend the physical and delve deeply into your lover's soul. Sharing intimate pleasures and confidences with your lover refreshes your body and renews your spirit. Once you get going, your amazing stamina keeps your bed partner satisfied all night long.

Sun in Scorpio/Mars in Gemini

You often feel torn between Gemini's love of personal freedom and Scorpio's jealousy and possessiveness. You long for the emotional security of a long-term union, but also crave variety, excitement, and change. Your sexuality is something of a puzzle, even to you. Sometimes sex is uppermost in your mind, and you just can't get enough. At other times you seem more interested in swapping ideas than kisses. A great communicator, you're as likely to channel your energy verbally as physically. You entice your lover with provocative erotic suggestions. Then, you follow up with the real thing.

Sun in Scorpio/Mars in Cancer

A loyal and devoted partner, you feel things deeply and, often come off as distant and mysterious. As a lover, you're sensual, romantic, demanding, and extraordinarily caring, sometimes to the point of obsession. The type of magnetism you project is powerful and alluring. Moreover, you thrive on a bit of intrigue and truly enjoy living on the edge. Even so, your approach to lovemaking is deliberately guarded until you're sure of your partner's feelings. Once involved, you're a sexual dynamo, and your physical prowess and emotional intensity make for thrilling bedroom encounters.

Sun in Scorpio/Mars in Leo

In love and romance, you're passionate, complex, and determined to have things your own way. Although fervently loyal, you can also be jealous and possessive. Sensuality and a fiery libido are your strengths and your weaknesses. The powerful combination of Mars in Leo's craving for attention and Sun in Scorpio's insatiable sexual appetite requires a hot-blooded, adoring bedmate. Your ideal partner openly appreciates your bedroom prowess, and makes a special effort to "seduce" you with fun toys and sexy, provocative apparel.

Sun in Scorpio/Mars in Virgo

Although you seem cooler and more intellectual than many Scorpios, in purely personal matters your actions are often based on instinct and emotion. However, your public discretion doesn't mean that you lack passion in private. Behind closed doors, you take your time, moving slowly and steadily toward intimacy. Your sensuality runs deep, and you believe that proper lovemaking is more than just technique. Nevertheless, Virgo's innate modesty makes it difficult for you to openly express your needs and desires in the bedroom. While overcoming your initial inhibitions can be challenging, with a partner you trust, vigorous lovemaking is cathartic and helps cement the loving bond between you.

Sun in Scorpio/Mars in Libra

Those born under this combination are more partnership-oriented than other Scorpios. But, despite your Sun sign's sexy image, you are discriminating when it comes to getting seriously involved. Nevertheless, when you find the one you consider your soul mate, you willingly pledge your undying devotion. With the right person in your bed, you are sensual, sensuous, romantic, daring, and sexually accommodating. However, if your love is rejected, or you feel betrayed, you're not likely to sit back and accept defeat graciously.

Sun in Scorpio/Mars in Scorpio

Since Scorpio is the sexiest sign in the zodiac, it should come as no surprise that sex is the natural milieu of double scorpions. With your animal magnetism and smoldering bedroom eyes, you're likely to attract plenty of admirers. An agile, accomplished lover, you possess a psychic-like intuition that allows you to tap into and satisfy your bedmate's deepest desires. However, you're interested in more than just physical lovemaking. You regard sex as a transcendent experience that allows you to merge with your partner on all levels: physical, mental, emotional, and spiritual.

Sun in Scorpio/Mars in Sagittarius

Sagittarius' adventurous nature makes you eager to expand your erotic horizons; however once you make a commitment, you stick with it. Despite

Scorpio's reputation for smoldering sexuality, you're capable of sublimating your strong physical desires when it suits your purposes. While you realize the potency of your magnetic sex appeal, you also understand the power of celibacy. In the bedroom and elsewhere, you have your own way of doing things. An air of mystery and secrecy guards your private feelings, so even your soul mate may have difficulty understanding what motivates you.

Sun in Scorpio/Mars in Capricorn

Although you come across as distant and mysterious, your ardent nature attracts suitors like a magnet. Your libido is red hot, but your courtship style is careful and cautious. However, once you find the love you seek, you're anything but shy. You expect to be the one calling the shots—in and out of the bedroom. Power and success act as aphrodisiacs for you, and you're drawn to partners who are as ambitious and capable as you. A born sensualist, your sexuality comes to life behind closed doors. Alone with your mate, you let down your guard, set aside daily cares, and surrender to your erotic desires.

Sun in Scorpio/Mars in Aquarius

Although you crave sexual fulfillment, you're really seeking a mental connection with your lover. Until then, you'd rather be master of your own destiny. While you may not be overly romantic, you are extraordinarily idealistic; for you love is meant to be a transcendent experience on all levels. However, your mood swings in the bedroom can be quite extreme. Your vacillation between Scorpio's passion and Aquarius's complete emotional detachment can drive your bed partner straight up the wall. The upshot is that your mate rarely knows where you are coming from or what you're thinking.

Sun in Scorpio/Mars in Pisces

You're highly sexed and extremely romantic, and love and intimacy play an important role in your life. However, while your angelic side seeks the ultimate in perfection, the devilish part of you longs to unravel the mysteries of a dark and dangerous love. You're also capable of displaying poignant vulnerability one moment, and becoming possessive and demanding the next. Still, you're more likely than other Scorpios to place your lover on a pedestal.

Combinations of the Sun in Sagittarius

Sun in Sagittarius/Mars in Aries

Few people know how to have a better time than you—in bed or out. You thrive on fun and excitement, and tempestuous affairs are your specialty. Since your capacity for boredom is extremely low, you're likely to stay around only as long as your partner holds your interest, but with the right person that could be a lifetime. You make love as passionately and exuberantly as you do everything else. Although happy enough to take the initiative, you appreciate a mate who is as bold and direct under the covers as you are.

Sun in Sagittarius/Mars in Taurus

Despite your desire to put down roots, you tend to become bored and restless when you stick close to home. Your ideal mate understands the restless side of your nature, and shares your love of excitement and adventure. Because of your desire for companionship, you're quicker to commit to a long-term relationship than other solar archers. You are highly sexed, and any gesture of physical contact with your lover is likely to spark your fire. Erotic touching energizes and incites your lusty libido. In bed, you respond amorously to the comfort and beauty of sumptuous surroundings and the tactile pleasure of silky, luxurious fabrics.

Sun in Sagittarius/Mars in Gemini

You are constantly on the lookout for new challenges and adventures and believe variety is the spice of life. This includes relationships, where you may garner a reputation as something of a romantic gypsy. Since you harbor a relaxed attitude toward love and companionship, too much intimacy or emotion tends to scare you off. Yet despite your freewheeling nature, you remain devoted to your family and close friends. In the bedroom, you pride yourself on spontaneity and creativity, and innovative, experimental sex is your forte. You're game to try just about anything at least once.

Sun in Sagittarius/Mars in Cancer

The term "delightful paradox" best describes your love nature. In social situations, your humor and easygoing nature make you a charming companion, but at home or work, your ambition comes to the forefront. In romance, you're carefree one moment and serious the next. A fiery sensuality simmers just below the surface of your reserve. Cautious at first, you slowly reveal the true extent of your passion and sensuality—with some encouragement. Your ideal bedmate grabs the initiative and "lures" you into uncharted sexual waters. Even if he or she proves less bold than you, sooner or later your lusty sexual appetite impels you toward more daring bedroom activities.

Sun in Sagittarius/Mars in Leo

Those born under this fiery combination think more with their hearts than their heads. In a romantic relationship, having a glorious time together is your top priority. Your bubbly enthusiasm and zest for life cause you to immerse yourself completely in everything you do. Sexually, you're passionate, energetic, uninhibited, and unpredictable. You fall in love easily and completely, and whirlwind romances are your specialty. You tend to get antsy if the relationship cools down, but you'll hang around as long as the sex is good. Although fervently loyal, you can also be jealous and possessive. While you treasure your own independence, you have difficulty granting equal freedom to your lover.

Sun in Sagittarius/Mars in Virgo

You are romantic, idealistic, and warmhearted, but critical of anyone who doesn't measure up to your high standards. You crave excitement, independence, and variety, but also the emotional security and stability of a permanent union. There is a touch of the conservative in you, and you need to find a way of reconciling the cautious side of your temperament with the sexy, adventurous part of your nature. In public, the virgin's reserve hides the archer's smoldering sexual desires. You long to explore various erotic practices with a lover you trust, but are too shy to come right out and say so. Although hesitant at first, with a little encouragement from a wise bed partner, your inherent inhibitions melt away to reveal a deep-seated, earthy sensuality.

Sun in Sagittarius/Mars in Libra

You believe that life is meant to be fun, and is much too short to be wasted on unhappiness. Your relaxed, easygoing nature prefers peace and serenity to the angst of emotional ups and downs. In an intimate union, you're a sexy bedmate who is more loving and affectionate than wildly passionate. The romantic inside you wants to be wooed and courted, not captured and caged. The harmonious ambiance of a tasteful décor puts you in the mood for lovemaking, and a partner with the aim to please and the ability to draw out your hidden passion turns you on.

Sun in Sagittarius/Mars in Scorpio

In an intimate relationship you're an ardent, generous, and demanding lover. Your solar archer is flirtatious and thrives on change and excitement, but you also have the loyalty and devotion of the scorpion. More passionate than romantic, you tend to be pretty direct about your sexual needs and preferences. Your ideal bed partner shares your adventurous nature as well as your desire to explore all facets of sexuality. Anything goes in your bedroom! You aren't interested in just the physical side of sex however; the emotional side matters as well.

Sun in Sagittarius/Mars in Sagittarius

Emotionally you're a paradox. On one hand, love is a grand and glorious adventure. On the other, loyalty and fidelity are difficult for you to sustain. Although your intentions are sincere, you lose interest once the initial excitement fades. In an intimate union, intellectual companionship counts as much as physical compatibility, and spontaneity and fun matter more to you than passion. In the bedroom or out, your approach to lovemaking is fun, wildly experimental, and geared toward new ways of expanding your sexual horizons. Spending time outdoors with your partner and making love under the stars invigorates you, and soothes your restless spirit.

Sun in Sagittarius/Mars in Capricorn

Typically, although you like the idea of a freewheeling lifestyle, you're more interested in the emotional security afforded by a long-term love union. In the bedroom, you're playful and teasing one moment, passionate and serious the next. You have a healthy appetite for sensual delights, and appreciate a lover who shares your interest in trying out various sexual techniques. You work hard, but when you play you're all about having fun. You're not afraid to throw caution to the winds and get off on experimenting with novel ways to enhance sexual pleasure with decadent edibles, naughty toys, and sexy bedroom attire.

Sun in Sagittarius/Mars in Aquarius

Although physically passionate, you're emotionally cooler than the average Sagittarian. You regard love as a glorious experience, but a roving eye and desire for personal freedom make fidelity difficult to sustain. Although no one will ever own you, a tolerant, understanding, considerate mate can win your love and loyalty. In the bedroom, you're open-minded and willing to try anything at least once. Even so, sex alone is rarely your number one consideration in a close relationship. Your brain is your ultimate erogenous zone. True love actually begins for you as a marriage of minds, only later progressing to a merging of physical bodies.

Sun in Sagittarius/Mars in Pisces

People with this combination are more emotional and less independent than other archers. You long to meet your soul mate, but have so much affection to give that your partner may not share the depths of emotion you feel. Moreover, if your lover falls short of your romantic ideal, you could be severely disappointed. However, when it comes to sex, you tend to be more pragmatic and, once sparked, your tireless libido spurs you on to exquisite intimacies. You use your unique combination of intuition and creativity to invent exotic ways to please and be pleased between the sheets. Inherently kind and caring, you're sensitive to your mate's needs and more than willing to satisfy them.

Combinations of the Sun in Capricorn

Sun in Capricorn/Mars in Aries

You appear cool on the surface, but are a true romantic and more emotional than other Capricorns. Dependable and loyal, you can also be moody and are not always the easiest person to live with. Your demanding nature makes you selective and your screening process for a perspective partner is more often ruled by your head than your heart. Nevertheless, once you make your choice, you move ahead with deliberate speed. Your libido is strong and your sexual energy high. In an intimate union you're a fiery lover with a straightforward seduction technique. Although reserved, behind closed doors your erotic sensuality quickly surfaces. You don't require a lot of foreplay to become physically aroused. In fact, you're usually willing to skip the appetizers and go directly to dessert.

Sun in Capricorn/Mars in Taurus

Your feelings run deep, yet you prefer to keep them hidden until you're sure of your partner's intentions. Beneath your restraint there is a smoldering sensuality, and you're an ardent, sexy lover in the privacy of the bedroom—where you like to be the one in charge. The intensity of your libido goes though cycles depending on your workload as you refuse to let anything or anyone distract you from your goals. You're most happy with a life partner who understands your shifting moods and shares your interests and ideas.

Sun in Capricorn/Mars in Gemini

You're ambitious, hardworking, and clever, and your fine mind, quick wit, and gift for gab make attracting potential suitors easy. In an intimate union, you're warm and loving physically, but emotionally inhibited; you're more comfortable talking about difficulties than dealing with the feelings they engender. Nevertheless, with a partner you trust, you reveal the passionate, randy side of your nature. You take great pride in your sexual prowess, and your bedroom is the perfect place for lusty lovemaking.

Sun in Capricorn/Mars in Cancer

Cancer is nurturing, demonstrative, and caring, but Capricorn is a cool customer not given to outward shows of affection; you may sometimes feel as if you're being pulled in two different directions at the same time. You don't like to appear vulnerable, and even in your most intimate relationships you need to know that you're the one in control. In bed, you like to take your time and build slowly to an all-encompassing passion. You enjoy pampering your lover, and expect to receive similar attention in return.

Sun in Capricorn/Mars in Leo

In love, you're passionate, generous, and loyal, but very demanding. Your proud nature and fragile ego require constant reassurance in the form of admiration and appreciation. Your sexy sensuality emerges behind closed doors. In the intimacy of a secure, loving relationship, you're ardent, romantic, and exceedingly generous. Once your physical passion is ignited, you reveal the red-hot desire that smolders beneath your controlled demeanor. Then you dazzle your lover with a combination of aggressive moves and slow, lingering impassioned caresses. You'll do everything possible to make sure all your partner's wishes are fulfilled.

Sun in Capricorn/Mars in Virgo

In relationships you're naturally shy and reserved, but when you feel secure and appreciated you make a caring and fun-loving—albeit critical and demanding—partner. Hiding beneath your stiff public persona, is a red-blooded, sensual lover, capable of intense passion. Your sex drive is strong and uncomplicated, and once you get past your fear of rejection, your bedroom approach is vigorous and straightforward. Sexually, you possess all the patience, vitality, and staying power typical of Capricorns. In the privacy of your bedroom, you expect your partner to be responsive and receptive to your need for lusty sex with a touch of racy playfulness. You don't require a great deal of foreplay, but after a hard day's work you enjoy a bit of indulgent pampering from your lover.

Sun in Capricorn/Mars in Libra

Relating comes naturally to Librans, and you may not feel complete without the companionship of a loving partner. However you need to be with someone who shares your interests and goals. You have a laid-back, but determined approach to lovemaking and take charge in a quiet, seductive way that leaves little room for doubt about your intentions. Your acute physical senses respond to beautiful surroundings, and a pleasant, graceful atmosphere turns you on. While you enjoy being admired, you're not especially free with flattery or compliments in return. Your ideal mate has the ability to see beneath the surface of your reserve to your true feelings.

Sun in Capricorn/Mars in Scorpio

This potent combination brings together sexy Scorpio's emotional intensity with the horny goat's legendary sexual prowess. In love and life, you know what you want and refuse to be sidetracked by extraneous circumstances. Despite your strong sex drive, you're a private and secretive person; what happens in the bedroom stays in the bedroom. Your seduction style is subtle, but powerful and your actions communicate what you can't say in words. You demand a lot from your bed partner—both physically and emotionally—and can be quite critical if he or she falls short of your expectations. Moreover, chemistry alone is not enough to entice you into an intimate union. To remain committed, you need a partner whose ideas and beliefs compliment your own.

Sun in Capricorn/Mars in Sagittarius

In personal relationships you're passionate and loving, but require more freedom than other solar Capricorns. Consequently, you respond more readily to an easygoing, relaxed approach to love and sex than to one that is exceedingly clingy or needy. Besides being affectionate and sexy, you have a humorous, whimsical side to your personality that makes you lots of fun to be with. In the bedroom, you're more open to alternative ideas and sexual experimentation than other goats. Given your love of nature and adventure, your favorite sexual playground may well be outdoors under the stars.

Sun in Capricorn/Mars in Capricorn

Seemingly fearless in your professional dealings, you often feel shy and insecure where your love life is concerned. Even so, you're a lusty creature with a deep need to love and be loved—although you'd rather die than admit it. Emotionally you're reserved, but are desirous and responsive in the bedroom. Highly sexed and swiftly aroused, your approach to lovemaking, while refined, is no-nonsense and direct. However, whatever you lack in the romance department, you more than make up for in skill—and sexual prowess.

Sun in Capricorn/Mars in Aquarius

Despite an apparently easygoing outer personality, there is a reserved inner goat standing guard over your privacy and independence. Since you like to maintain a certain amount of emotional distance, you rarely allow anyone to get too close to you. Sexually, however, you're open-minded and more unconventional than other Capricorns, but you sometimes get so caught up in other things that you forget about lovemaking altogether. However, it usually only takes a little reminder to spark your latent desire and when you relax, your innate passion and sensuality emerge. With a few sexy suggestions to get you started, you quickly become a spirited, inventive lover.

Sun in Capricorn/Mars in Pisces

More tenderhearted and romantic than the typical goat, you can also be as controlling and demanding as any other Capricorn. You're genuinely devoted to your partner, and will even sacrifice your own interests in favor of your beloved. A considerate lover, you're prepared to do whatever it takes to keep your partner happy. No one would call you kinky, but you're flexible, open-minded, and willing to please. For you, being in love is the ultimate turn-on, but since your imagination is your major erotic zone, too much reality can be a real downer.

Combinations of the Sun in Aquarius

Sun in Aquarius/Mars in Aries

There is precious little that is conventional in your makeup. Naturally impulsive and rebellious in all life areas, you push the envelope of your innovative ideas to their furthest edge. You don't go by other people's rules, and don't expect them to follow yours. When choosing a partner, you consider fun and companionship to be as important as sexual compatibility. Even so, your sexuality is passionate and straightforward, and you thoroughly enjoy making love—even though there are times when your libido requires a wake-up call. Since your bedroom responses hinge on mental stimulation, a gentle reminder of what you've been missing is usually all it takes to reignite your sexual fire.

Sun in Aquarius/Mars in Taurus

You're more solid and dependable than other Aquarians, and a long-term relationship appeals to you on many levels. Upfront and direct about your sexual impulses, you have no compunction about initiating daring and experimental lovemaking when the mood is upon you. At your best, you are an exciting, innovative bedmate. Yet despite your lack of regard for what society considers proper behavior, you're a genuine romantic and need more from your lover than just sex.

Sun in Aquarius/Mars in Gemini

Despite being a zealous, exhilarating, creative lover, you tend not to take lovemaking too seriously; sex for you is mainly fun and games. In bed and out, you thrive on variety and experimentation and have a very low tolerance for dull sexual routine. More verbal than sensual, words stimulate your physical desires in ways that even the most erotic touching cannot accomplish. The more you talk about what you'd like to do or have done to you, the more sexually turned on you become. You're quite comfortable discussing sex, yet clam up when it comes to talking about feelings and emotions.

Sun in Aquarius/Mars in Cancer

Aquarian detachment veils your deep devotion to your family and friends and, in intimate relationships, you often feel conflicted between the desire for freedom mandated by Aquarius, and Cancer's need for stability and security. More conservative than the typical water bearer, you're also considerably more passionate and your quirky sexual nature readily asserts itself behind closed doors. As a result, your approach to lovemaking alternates between innovative and experimental and traditionally romantic. Your attitude toward erotica is nonjudgmental. Agreeable and eager to please in the bedroom, you first find out what your partner likes and then you provide it.

Sun in Aquarius/Mars in Leo

When you love, you love with your whole heart and don't tolerate deception or deceit. Your close relationships have to be on your terms, and you swiftly lose interest in anyone with whom you have no intellectual connection. Not even your dearest love can get away with telling you what to do, but you make a loyal, loving partner. Even though you're capable of intense passion, there is a playful, mischievous side to your nature that allows you to have a great deal of fun in bed. Moreover, your innate curiosity makes you want to try new things and you're not afraid to venture into previously unexplored sexual territory.

Sun in Aquarius/Mars in Virgo

Outwardly, you tend to appear cool and disinterested in intimacy, but on the inside you're very much in need of love and affection. Because you believe the heart should rule the head, you're more comfortable analyzing and categorizing your feelings than experiencing them. Emotionally, you fear too much intimacy, but physically you're open to just about anything that brings pleasure to both parties. Behind closed doors, you're warm, witty, and extremely sexy—and have a free, uninhibited approach to lovemaking that leads to hours of fun and flirtation. However, you require an intellectual connection along with the physical one; when your mind is turned on, your body will soon follow.

Sun in Aquarius/Mars in Libra

Those born under this combination are generally more romantic and partnership-minded than other Aquarians. Even so, you wouldn't dream of surrendering your cherished independence for a relationship that doesn't live up to your extremely high standards. Your ideal love combines sex and romance with friendship and mental rapport. In the bedroom, Libra's delicacy and sophistication adds beauty and romance to Aquarius's intellectual style of lovemaking. Pleasing your lover is all-important for you and, with a like-minded partner, you're predisposed to try any position or erotic toy at least once.

Sun in Aquarius/Mars in Scorpio

Aquarius's relaxed attitude toward love and sex just doesn't mesh well with the intensity of the scorpion's secretive, all-or-nothing approach to intimate relationships. Moreover, your feelings of being misunderstood make you wary of commitment. In the bedroom, you are an inventive and enthusiastic lover, but often feel conflicted between your intellectual awareness of sex as a physical act, and your emotional ideal of lovemaking as a transcendent union. As a result, you may be wildly passionate one day and seemingly disinterested the next.

Sun in Aquarius/Mars in Sagittarius

Both your Sun and Mars signs incline toward wariness of any commitment that curbs your ability to move around without restraint. No matter how close you get to your mate, there's always a part of you that you reserve solely for yourself. In the bedroom, you're an innovative, fiery, and enthusiastic lover. Although you regard sex as extremely liberating, pleasurable, and fun, for you, a long-term relationship should be based on common interests and ideals, and the sharing of a larger purpose.

Sun in Aquarius/Mars in Capricorn

Despite Capricorn's ingrained respect for tradition, Aquarius gives you a freer, more unconventional outlook with regard to your intimate relationships. Even so, you'll eventually have to choose between independence and commitment. Your strong sex drive notwithstanding, at times you may repress or ignore your physical needs. However, when you stop trying to control and analyze your feelings, and give into your sexual impulses, you're a passionate, enthusiastic, and exceedingly sensual lover. For you, physical stimulation begins in the imagination, and you're seduced more readily with sensuous elegance and sophistication than with overt displays of eroticism.

Sun in Aquarius/Mars in Aquarius

Inherently self-motivated and somewhat eccentric, you have little patience with society's rules and regulations. In an intimate union, you want a relationship that's solidly based in companionship, friendship, and common interests. In the bedroom, you exist in a brave new world of possibilities. You believe that nothing is too far out of the realm of possibility between the sheets—as long as both partners are satisfied. However, since you rationalize everything, including your emotions, you never lose control or allow yourself to be swept away by passion.

Sun in Aquarius/Mars in Pisces

You go back and forth between Aquarius's detachment and desire for independence, and Pisces' longing to establish an intense connection with a soul mate; you yearn for intimacy, but are afraid of entrapment and emotional vulnerability. However, once you overcome your reservations about intimacy, you throw yourself into lovemaking with breathtaking intensity—and won't stop until both you and your lover are spent. A romantic seduction scene, with soft music and sexy apparel gets your motor running.

Combinations of the Sun in Pisces

Sun in Pisces/Mars in Aries

Although you yearn for the bliss of a perfect union with your true love, once you get it the passive-aggressive characteristic in your nature can make it difficult for you to hold onto the intimacy and emotional support you crave. Naturally sensuous, with a strong sex drive, you are an eager, dynamic lover, but imaginary role-playing games just don't do it for you. Instead, you're turned on by the real thing, starting with a romantic candlelit dinner and culminating in spicy, erotic, all-night lovemaking.

Sun in Pisces/Mars in Taurus

A true romantic, you enjoy courting and being courted and as long as you feel secure in a relationship, you're a wonderful, caring, considerate partner. However, when your sensitive feelings are hurt, you turn clingy and possessive. For you lovemaking is a total experience, and you expect the sex act to be physically and emotionally satisfying for both partners. Moreover, you project an extremely seductive air of mystery and vulnerability. Yet, despite your delicate sensibilities, there is nothing prissy about you. In the privacy of the bedroom you're sensual and extremely uninhibited. When the lights turn off, you turn on.

Sun in Pisces/Mars in Gemini

Sociable, outgoing, and witty, you want a partner who provides intellectual stimulation along with love and companionship. Even though you yearn for the grounding of a stable union, a part of you fears commitment. In the bedroom, you're sensual and alluring. A skillful lover and compulsive charmer, your technique is a mixture of tenderness and sexual expertise. You have few inhibitions, and dislike having your activities confined to a specific time or place. Sexy talk turns you on, and your idea of great foreplay combines kissing and stroking with lively, flirtatious sexual banter.

Sun in Pisces/Mars in Cancer

In matters of the heart, you're a total romantic and, in an intimate union, you're caring and protective of your beloved. To you, sex and sensuality are part of the entire package that makes up any romantic alliance; you crave emotional fulfillment along with physical gratification. In a subtle, unobtrusive way, you control and direct much of the bedroom activity. Moreover, you captivate and enchant your lover with a unique combination of alluring fantasy and red-hot reality. Once trust is established, you're capable of letting go completely and losing yourself in the wild expanse of desire generated by your love and fiery passion.

Sun in Pisces/Mars in Leo

You radiate a magical seduction that draws love and romance into your life. Fiercely loyal, intense, and sensitive, you pour yourself heart and soul into an intimate union. Your idealistic attitude toward romance leads you to expect a lot of give and take in the bedroom, and you're as sensitive to your lovers' needs as you are to your own. You're an innovative and creative bedmate, particularly with a partner who makes you feel loved and admired. Nevertheless, unless you experience the intensity of true love, you won't feel emotionally or physically satisfied.

Sun in Pisces/Mars in Virgo

A gentle, caring bed partner, your approach to lovemaking is tender yet subtly seductive. Intuitive by nature, you pick up on your significant other's needs, in and out of the bedroom. Making your lover feel cherished and appreciated is your special talent and, while you'd never say so, you expect the same kind of consideration in return. You regard physical love as an expression of deeper feelings—a mingling of body, mind, and soul. You're turned on by the romance of poetry and music, and by dreamy moments of intimacy with your beloved.

Sun in Pisces/Mars in Libra

You don't like being alone, but your ideas regarding long-term unions tend to be unrealistic. Sometimes you become so devoted to pleasing your lover, that you forget that the relationship is meant to be an equal partnership. Caring, versatile, and highly skilled in lovemaking, you're as readily aroused by giving as receiving pleasure. Although you find foreplay a wonderful turn-on, a more direct path to your sensual side is through your intellect and imagination. You want to be with a lover who knows how to excite your mind along with your body.

Sun in Pisces/Mars in Scorpio

With your strong intuition and vivid imagination, all things strange, mysterious, unknown, and unknowable your fascinated by. Close relationships are really important to you, and intimacy—or its lack—has a huge impact on your life. As a result, your romantic alliances are often as dramatic and turbulent as they are intense. You may display a poignant vulnerability one moment, then become jealous, possessive, and demanding the next. In the bedroom, you intuit the best and most effective way to arouse and enchant your lover. You're more than capable when it comes to devising erotic delights to keep your lover satisfied. Sharing steamy pleasures with your partner sparks your own desires and spurs you on to even more passionate lovemaking.

Sun in Pisces/Mars in Sagittarius

Sun in Pisces is romantic, but not aggressive with regard to love and sex. Mars in Sagittarius, on the other hand, tends to be boldly direct and upfront about everything related to sexuality. In the bedroom, your changeable nature makes you appear shy and hesitant one moment, spontaneous and uninhibited the next. Either way, imagination plays a huge part in your love life and you yearn to be swept away on a wave of ecstasy. A dreamy atmosphere where you share moments of exquisite intimacy arouses you, and enhances your sensual pleasure. You enjoy using your innate creativity to devise exotic scenarios to play out with your partner.

Sun in Pisces/Mars in Capricorn

Behind your serious facade, there is a whimsical, humorous side to your personality that makes you a great deal of fun to be with. In your love life, you come off as self-contained, but you actually crave love and affection. Behind closed doors, you're a carnal, sexy, and generous lover. You intuit your partner's unspoken desires and instinctively respond to them. Even so, spontaneity is not your style. You don't much care for unplanned encounters, preferring instead to set up "sex dates" in advance.

Sun in Pisces/Mars in Aquarius

In intimate relationships you are as loving, caring, and considerate as other Pisces, but Aquarius makes you more independent than the typical solar fish. Your ideal mate is the one who understands your need for "alone time" to explore your personal interests. You expect more than sex and romance from a love relationship; you're really seeking a psychic link that transcends differences in personality and temperament. The idea of exploring outrageous sexual fantasies appeals to you. You'll dress up for role-playing games or experiment with different positions, as long as your bed partner is agreeable.

Sun in Pisces/Mars in Pisces

Love is one of the few necessities in your life and your sexuality is closely allied to your dreams and imagination. When you fall in love, you fall hook, line, and sinker. While not sexually aggressive, your bedroom allure is right up there with the most seductive in the zodiac. In bed and out, you put your partner's desires ahead of your own and will do just about anything to keep him or her happy. Although fear of rejection may make you reluctant to initiate the first move, you telegraph your own desires so completely that even the most insensitive lover has little trouble getting the message.

part 2

MOON AND VENUS: YOUR LOVE NATURE

The Moon in the horoscope symbolizes emotional reactions and has a lot to do with your responses to love and affection. Its sign in the birth chart indicates the ways you're likely to react in an intimate union. Venus, the embodiment of romantic love and physical attraction, indicates your attitude toward close relationships, how you express (or repress) your romantic feelings, what you are seeking from a partner, and what you expect to give in return.

In combination, the signs that the Moon and Venus occupy in your birth chart reveal your emotional strengths and insecurities, the role love plays in your life, how you go about attracting a lover, and how you're likely to behave within the context of a romantic relationship.

4

Moon

THE MOON SHINES BECAUSE IT REFLECTS THE SUN'S LIGHT; it actually emits no light of its own. In spite of its reflected glory, the Moon has been personified as the "Queen of the Night," and revered throughout history. Observance of the Moon's waxing and waning inspired both awe and fear, especially during the dark period when the Moon disappears from view for three nights. Nearly everywhere in the ancient world, connections were made between the Moon's phases, the rhythm of nature, and the lives of human beings. In some places the phases were related to menstruation, sexual intercourse, pregnancy, and delivery, in others childhood, maturity, death, and rebirth.

The Moon's position in the natal chart is extremely significant and, in Western astrology, the Moon's placement is ranked second in importance to that of the Sun. Your birth Moon shows the ways in which you express and deal with your feelings, and describes your inner nature and interior hidden self. (If you're not sure what your Moon Sign is, use the tables in Appendix B to determine it.) The domain of the Moon is the subconscious mind and its relationship to emotions, instincts, habits, intuition, psychic ability, dreams, and memories. Because the Moon influences your deepest thoughts and fantasies and illuminates your innermost feelings, its sign shows what you really care about in life, and what you will be happiest doing or being. The Moon's dominion includes women, conception, pregnancy, birth, childhood experience, emotional security, home, family, and the public.

Like Sun signs, Moon signs—discussed in detail in this chapter—are grouped by the three qualities of being (Cardinal, Fixed, Mutable) and the four Elements (Fire, Earth, Air, Water) described in Chapter 1.

Moon in Aries

In fiery Aries, the Moon's energy is dynamic and impulsive. Thrilled by adventure, opportunity, and challenging situations, you can usually be found in the forefront of any new activity. A natural rebel, you prefer making your own rules to living under other people's restrictions. Since you don't much care about any opinions other than your own, you don't seek advice, and rarely follow it if offered.

Diplomacy is not your strong suit; you generally come right out and say whatever you're thinking. Moon in Aries is never secretive or deceitful, preferring unvarnished truth to sugarcoated deception. You deal with things immediately, often with little thought, but always with tremendous energy and verve. Possessing great charm and wit, you exude an infectious optimism that's not always justified. Even so, you're a natural leader and something of a visionary. Those around you easily get caught up in your enthusiasms, sometimes even to the point of joining in your madcap schemes.

In Bed

Aries' passion is immediate; love and desire do not build up gradually, but begin full force and proceed with high intensity. In the bedroom, you enjoy taking the lead, and go after what you want with intensity and determination. Between the sheets you're a fiery lover—easily aroused, with physical desires that urgently demand satisfaction. You have a strong appetite for anything new and innovative, and a talent for keeping the spirit of your love alive and thriving. You're open to trying anything that is fun and adventurous—at least once.

Although your sexual needs are high, intimate involvement with one person may become a source of conflict, because you require a great deal of personal freedom. It's often easier for you to commit yourself physically than emotionally, so you deflect what you're feeling into your sexuality. Then you deal with your emotions on that level, instead of confronting them directly. For you, a successful permanent relationship needs to be based in friendship as well as in love and romance.

Moon in Taurus

This Moon sign emphasizes the material side of life, and you enjoy all of its pleasures including lovemaking, good food and drink, art and music, and relaxing in pleasant surroundings. Sensual and romantic, Moon in Taurus thrives on physical contact and no lover of yours will want for attention. Bulls are herd animals, and you enjoy being surrounded by family members, friends, and acquaintances with whom you are warm and demonstrative.

Your basic temperament is serene and passive, and you'll go out of your way to avoid rocking the boat. You believe in loving, not fighting, but repeated hassling can turn you into the proverbial Raging Bull. With your proud nature, it's difficult for you deal with slights and rejection. Bulls may forgive, but they rarely forget. Your propensity for bearing grudges makes you waste precious time and energy by doggedly hanging on to old resentments.

In Bed

Your needs and desires are simple and of a practical, physical nature. Highly physical, your enjoyment of lovemaking is direct and unabashed and all types of physical contact appeal to your strongly sensuous nature. While you have no trouble drawing your lover to you, you actually enjoy being seduced. Initially shy, you become a sexual dynamo once aroused. For Taurus the neck is a major erogenous zone, and you welcome slow, sliding kisses along your neck as a prelude to lovemaking. Your personal recipe for love consists of equal parts passion and romance.

However, while romantic, you don't overlook the realities of life. No matter how passionate, hasty couplings in bleak, uncomfortable places hold little appeal for you. The bed partner who sets the scene with candles, music, and flowers, and plies you with delectable goodies such as exotic fruits, chocolates, and fine wines truly knows the surest way to your heart.

Moon in Gemini

In airy Gemini, the Moon's energy is scattered and erratic, making you moody, restless, and high-strung. Curious and questioning, you're continually on the lookout for new types of intellectual stimulation; you take a lively interest in everything you see and everyone you meet. However, you have a short attention span, and tend to flit from interest to interest, without taking the time to probe the depths of any one subject.

You possess a carefree, easygoing manner, razor-sharp wit, and gift for gab that makes you a popular, sought after companion. You reflect the mood of those around you, and respond to situations the way you think others expect you to respond. By saying what people want to hear, instead of revealing your own opinions, you give the appearance of emotional noninvolvement. It is not surprising, then, that others have difficulty getting to know the real you.

In Bed

More mental than emotional or physical, your major erotic zone is between your ears. You get off on fantasizing and talking about sex. Your aversion to boredom makes witty banter and subtle promises of previously untried bedroom techniques the ideal come-on from a prospective lover. You expect sex to be fun and prefer making love in unusual places. Risk provides an added thrill, and the possibility of getting caught in the act fuels your erotic imaginings. Even at home, you dislike having your lovemaking confined to the bedroom. Variety and change stimulate your desires, and you're willing to try anything new or different. Since you love gadgets, sex toys and devices are a welcome addition to your erotic activities.

Moon in Cancer

Lunar crabs are some of the most emotional members of the zodiacal family and the most easily wounded by perceived slights and rebuffs. You tend to be strongly impressionable, with an artistic temperament that works best when allowed to function at its own pace. You're extremely self-protective and rarely show your emotions openly, preferring to hide your vulnerability behind a protective facade. Suspicious of the motives of others, you trust your own feelings and hunches. Your intuition is keen, and you usually rely on it. However, when you allow your heart to rule your head, you have great difficulty making rational, detached decisions.

In Bed

In an intimate union, the intensity of your sexuality is directly connected to the depth of your feeling for your companion. The act of love can carry you to incredible heights or leave you feeling deflated and let down. Sex for its own sake is just not your style. In the bedroom, your approach is romantic, sensual, tender, and always considerate of your lover's wishes.

You long to be courted and love to kiss and cuddle between the sheets. In intimate moments, you're shy and sensitive, but in your dreams, you're bold, imaginative, and audacious enough to take risks that you hesitate to pursue in reality. Your ideal bed partner coaxes you out of your shell, and gets you to reveal your most erotic imaginings. When acting out your secret fantasies, you engage your entire being in an exotic game of joyful seduction.

Moon in Leo

In Leo the Moon's power is positive and upbeat, and even its shadowy side is less dark than in other signs. Moon in Leos command respect, and are typically optimistic and ambitious with an instinctive urge to rule. Naturally extroverted and dramatic, your warm, generous nature wins people over, and your easygoing charm and wonderful sense of humor keep them interested and entertained.

The typical lunar lion projects an air of supreme self-confidence, but is prone to self-doubt and requires repeated positive reinforcement. Your beliefs and ideas are directly tied to your feelings and emotions. When there is a conflict between your head and heart, you usually follow your heart. Your enthusiastic nature is prone to exaggeration, and a tendency to say more than you mean can make you appear thoughtless or insincere.

In Bed

Love is your ultimate aphrodisiac, and your idea of the perfect turn-on includes tons of affection and admiration. As a lover, you're not a big fan of subtlety and believe that actions really do speak louder than words. While aggressive and dramatic in the bedroom, you're never crude or boorish. Your sunny, romantic idealism permeates your lovemaking just as it lights up every other area of your life.

Physical intimacy makes you feel alive and fulfilled, and your sexual prowess and ability to please your lover are exceedingly important to you. Because your pleasure-seeking instincts are strong, you're eager to experience all the joys lovemaking has to offer. Your sex drive is greatly enhanced by the comfortable accoutrements of the good life, and you get off on being pampered and wooed luxuriously, as befits your regal, leonine status.

Moon in Virgo

People born under this Moon sign rely more on intellectual analysis than emotion or intuition. Reason is your god, and you trust it over all else. However, this can make it difficult for you to express what you feel, making you come across as cold, detached, or prudish, when you're actually thin-skinned and easily hurt. There is a strong link between your emotions, and your physical body; the stress of existing in a world that doesn't live up to your ideal of perfection can lead to health problems.

Uncomfortable unless you can figure things out for yourself, you feel safest when you're able to analyze, categorize, organize, and understand everything in your environment. Never one to suffer fools gladly, you find it especially frustrating when forced to deal with individuals who you consider lazy, illogical, or scatterbrained.

In Bed

Because of its introverted aspect, Virgo is not a very sexual position for the Moon. Even when your deepest feelings are engaged, your shyness makes it hard for you to be demonstrative. You want a close union based on mutual respect and affection, and appreciate the refined elegance of beautiful, tasteful surroundings. Getting physical with your lover allows you to relax and forget about mundane worries. Since pleasing your mate is foremost in your mind, once you feel comfortable with your bedmate you make an amazingly skilled, generous bed partner. When you find a new way to gratify your lover, you hone the technique until it approaches perfection. While not the most exciting lover, you're definitely one of the most considerate and obliging. Moreover, like a fine wine, your sensuality becomes richer with age and experience.

Moon in Libra

Luna Libra's zodiacal role is that of mediator and peacemaker. Given your strong need for harmony and approbation, some may consider you an easy target. However, despite your amiability and aversion to disputes, you're no pushover. Instead of arguing, you get all the facts and use your tact and diplomacy to sway potential combatants and win them over to your point of view.

The dark side of this Moon sign usually manifests as procrastination and fence sitting. You're so good at weighing the merits of each side of an argument that you often find it impossible to come to a concrete conclusion. This may make you appear wishy-washy, but the truth is that you hate to think your decision could cause dissention and disharmony. You want to please everyone, but must ultimately realize that it's impossible to be all things to all people.

In Bed

Your approach to lovemaking is glamorous and alluring. You appreciate the intricate rituals of old-fashioned courtship, and enjoy being wooed with finesse and sophistication. Sex and romance are intertwined in your mind, and you prefer artful seduction to a carnal free-for-all. Your erotic sensuality emerges most readily in a sumptuous setting that engages all the senses. Luxurious bedding, sultry nightwear, soft music, flickering candles, and fresh flowers add the requisite spice to your lovemaking. A special night dedicated to love, in a romantic setting with moonlight and whispered words of adoration, serves as a genuine turn-on and affectionate gestures and loving words draw out your passions and get your sexual juices flowing.

Moon in Scorpio

This is a difficult placement, because lunar scorpions are capable of concentrating their energies and focusing on their objectives with a passion that sometimes approaches obsession. Always interested in what lies beneath the surface, your instinctive urge is to keep digging until you get to the bottom of things. Despite this, Scorpios are very good at hiding their deepest feelings; you may be pathological in your secretiveness, never revealing yourself entirely to another person. Inclined to bottle up most of your disappointments, you may become silent and withdrawn if you feel unable to control or change what you don't like. Eventually, pent up frustration can surface as angry outbursts that affect your work, health, and relationships, but Moon in Scorpios are unsurpassed when it comes to bouncing back from disappointment, illness, and in some cases the threshold of death's door.

In Bed

Imbued with a smoldering sexuality, when you turn on your sultry charm, few can resist you and, once you get going beneath the covers, you have tremendous staying power. Your passionate lovemaking requires a dynamic bed partner with physical stamina equal to your own. Your innate fascination with sexuality inspires numerous fantasies of erotic seduction. Acting out these scenarios with your mate provides an outlet for your active imagination in addition to being a guaranteed turn-on. An extremist, you equate sex with power and control, making you a demanding, but wickedly delightful lover. You intuit your partner's secret desires—and make them come true. Sharing your lusty thoughts with your beloved serves as tantalizing foreplay for steamy nights of intense lovemaking.

Moon in Sagittarius

People with the Moon in this sign are restless in mind and body. A nature lover, you thrive on exercise and constant activity. Affectionate, outgoing, and sociable, you have many friends and acquaintances. However, you require a great deal of freedom to follow your dreams and too much togetherness scares you. With your adventurous nature urging you forward, you may change directions many times during your life, but you always know who you are and where you're headed. Autonomous and independent, you rarely ask for or follow the advice of other people. However, you're not above giving advice to others, whether or not they want to hear it. You tend to be overly candid, especially in situations where a more diplomatic approach would be preferable.

In Bed

Your sex drive is strong, but erratic. At times, your bedroom style can be wildly experimental, and you're always eager to explore new ways of expanding your sensual horizons. Physical attraction sparks your interest initially, but it takes intellectual stimulation to hold it indefinitely. Spontaneity, fun, excitement, and adventure turn you on and matter more to you than grand passion. A short getaway is relaxing, and camping, hiking, and making love under the stars reinvigorates you.

Your natural exuberance, candor, and lack of guile in the bedroom allow you to express your sexual desires openly. More interested in action than fantasy, having sex in different locations—at home and otherwise—is a real turn-on for you. Why be restricted to the bedroom when there are so many other appealing places to make love?

Moon in Capricorn

The sensitive, ever-changing Moon is uncomfortable in Capricorn's controlled environment of rules and regulations and the person born under this placement is typically serious, industrious, and ambitious, with a tendency to put practical considerations ahead of emotional ones. Naturally reserved and reticent, you rarely appear relaxed and comfortable within yourself.

Trust doesn't come easily to you, and your emotional insecurities cause you to build walls between yourself and others. When feeling insecure, you typically take over and assume control of the situation. You find safety and security in structure, routine, and strictly drawn boundaries. In a crisis, you inevitably turn to the safety of hard work and well-defined routines to help get you through.

In Bed

When aroused the strongly sexed lunar goat is capable of intense and sustained ardor. Where lovemaking is concerned, you like to take it slow and get it right and you work at love with the same diligence and dedication that you apply to other areas of your life. Your style of lovemaking, while respectful and refined, tends to be no-nonsense and you consider coquettish games a waste of time. Nevertheless, whatever you lack in the romance department, you more than make up for in skill and sexual prowess. Despite your down-to-earth attitude toward sexuality, you can be vamped and seduced. Your ideal lover knows how to lure the horny goat out of hiding by creating an atmosphere of sensuality where you can relax and give full rein to your many erotic desires.

Moon in Aquarius

The individual born under this sign is cool-headed and cerebral and tends to distrust emotions as being messy and irrational. Strong feelings such as anger and jealousy make you uncomfortable and, though outwardly friendly, at heart you're somewhat of a loner. Aquarians "feel" with their minds, and your inclination is to deny or repress emotions instead of dealing with them directly. Your unconventional outlook and eccentric behavior make it difficult for you to fit in, and at times you suffer from loneliness and a sense of detachment from the world around you. Adept at analyzing everyone else's motivations, you're often totally clueless where your own are concerned.

In Bed

In the bedroom, you're daring and unconventional. A genuine nonconformist, you're sexually uninhibited and predisposed to experimentation; if something sounds fun, you're willing to give it a go. You exude a sex appeal that positively crackles with electricity, and you believe that nothing is too far out as long as it pleases both partners. However, no matter how much you enjoy making love, you always keep your wits about you and never allow yourself to be totally swept away by passion. Lovemaking has little meaning for you unless it truly engages your mind along with your body, and you respond as readily to verbal suggestion as to physical stimulation.

Moon in Pisces

The lunar fish is perceived as the archetypal dreamer of the zodiac and, much of the time, you inhabit a fantasy world of your own creation. Romantic and idealistic in the extreme, you'd rather contemplate life through a pair of rose-colored glasses, than deal with its harsh realities. Yours is the most compassionate of the Moon signs, and you find it virtually impossible to detach emotionally from the problems and difficulties of others. You soak up other people's emotions, and feel what they feel. Unfortunately, sometimes you can't tell the difference between your own feelings and what you're picking up from others. When this happens, you can suddenly become moody, disturbed, or unhappy without knowing why.

In Bed

For the fish, love and sex are irrevocably intertwined, and nothing gets your attention faster than an old-fashioned romantic courtship. You want a lover who quotes poetry, scatters rose petals, and makes all-consuming love by candlelight. In turn, you enchant your lover through subtle seduction, and your unpredictable nature makes you endlessly fascinating. In bed, your aura of vulnerability brings out your partner's protective instincts. Although you love to kiss and cuddle, the physical side of sex matters less to you than an emotional connection with your lover. Even so, you're no slouch between the sheets. Prepared to give your all, you readily set your own needs and desires aside in order to satisfy those of your bedmate.

5

Venus

AFTER THE SUN AND MOON, THE BRIGHT, BEAUTIFUL PLANET VENUS—known as the "morning and evening star" because it's the first to appear in the night sky and the last to disappear at dawn—is our most noticeable celestial body. Venus, or Aphrodite, was the Greek goddess of love and beauty who mischievously complicated and controlled everyone's love life. Though married, sensual Venus's affections could not be contained to only one relationship, and she spread her favors liberally among both gods and mortals. In classical astrology, the zodiacal sign Libra is the masculine or day phase of Venus, and Taurus is its feminine or night phase.

Venus in the birth chart represents affection, happiness, pleasure, abundance, and the desire for intimacy with another person. If you don't know your Venus sign, you can find it by looking it up in Appendix C: Mars and Venus Ephemeris Tables. The key Venusian qualities are peace, beauty, harmony, artistic sensibility, charm, graciousness, diplomacy, sensuality, romance, and femininity. Venus is closely connected to your love, nature, aesthetic sensibilities, and sense of values.

The way Venus manifests itself in your chart—as detailed throughout this chapter—is a clear indicator of what gives you joy and pleasure during lovemaking. Your Venus sign defines the various ways in which you express your sensuality, attract love and affection, and go about satisfying your lover's needs and desires. Whereas Mars is associated with passion, lust, and conquest, the sexuality of Venus is seductive, erotic, and denotes friendship, compassion, and understanding between lovers.

Venus in Aries

With this placement of Venus, you're assertive, enthusiastic, self-expressive, creative, and cheerful. You crave excitement and adventure in all areas of your life and sex and romance are equally important for you. However, Aries is impulsive and hopelessly addicted to conquest while Venus falls in and out of love quickly. The result of this mix is often a lack of foresight and some instability where long-term unions are concerned.

Naturally cheerful and upbeat, you exude charm and charisma in social situations. Innately daring and flirtatious, you're competitive when seeking the attentions and affections of a potential lover. Because you view romantic involvement as a competition to be won, you become irritable and moody when you lose. You pursue a lover ardently and impulsively—and sometimes your initial zeal can lead you into fly-by-night affairs. You don't like anything that's too settled or routine and, more than anything else, you require excitement, challenge, and constant mental and physical stimulation in an intimate relationship.

Venus in Taurus

The Fixed-natured Venusian bull needs a certain measure of predictability and dependability in a romantic relationship, and when you fall in love, it's typically permanent and enduring. A materialist who dislikes disruption and upheaval, you resist change of any kind and require a deep commitment from your partner. Once you find the person you want, you grab on with both hands and refuse to let go without a struggle. If your intimate relationship comes to an end, it's probably your partner doing the leaving.

Thanks to your deep appreciation of the physical world and its pleasures, you experience love in a straightforward, sensual, tactile manner and expect hands-on expressions of warmth and affection in the bedroom. You enjoy good sex in the same way that you take pleasure in good food and drink, luxurious surroundings, and beautiful things. Easygoing and cheerful, you like to have a good time and help others do the same. If your mate has any complaints, it could be that you can get a little too comfortable and settled in your relationship. However, despite your loyalty, generosity, and faithfulness, you can put your lover through the ringer with your jealousy.

Venus in Gemini

Driven by a powerful intellectual curiosity, a restless nature, and a diversity of interests, you long to sample everything life has to offer. You have an excitable, childlike attitude toward romance, approaching new affairs with optimism and high expectations. Consequently, your romantic encounters may be many and brief before you finally decide to settle down. Since your romantic feelings are neither deep nor intense, you tend to bounce back quickly from disappointments in love. For you, mental stimulation and the simple joy of being together are absolute musts for any alliance to have a chance of becoming permanent.

Good communication is of the utmost importance; without it no amount of sexual attraction will hold your interest. You need a mate with whom you can discuss your varied interests and share your thoughts and ideas. However, though willing to talk endlessly about your relationship, you're inclined to gloss over most of the deeper emotional issues. In love, as in life, your tastes change often, and it can be hard for your significant other to know what to expect from one day, or even one hour, to the next.

Venus in Cancer

In an intimate union, you show your love by nurturing and caring for your mate, and expect the same in return. Venus in Cancer is super sensitive, and you tend to be more than a little moody where love is concerned. Since you rank among the most psychic of lovers, you pay more attention to your partner's feelings than his or her words. Consequently real or imagined slights can prompt you to retreat into your crab shell. Ever fearful of rejection, you know that you're easily hurt and want to protect yourself at all times Romantic by nature, sincerity from your partner is important to you, and you're likely to be attracted to people who are genuine in their affections. The suitor who knows how to make you feel secure and well cared for will be rewarded with an affectionate, patient, dependable, and loving life partner.

Venus in Leo

Venus in Leo is dramatic, enthusiastic, and self-confident, and glamour, excitement, and charm mark your courting style. A born showperson, with tons of physical and emotional magnetism, you enjoy being noticed and popular. Romance helps you maintain your high opinion of yourself, and you're happiest when in love. In an intimate union you're lavish with your attentions, presents, and with yourself. Leo is a Fixed sign, and despite all the fun and showmanship, you're an extremely stable, loyal, and faithful partner.

Venusian lions make passionate, ardent lovers, and your affection is sincere and wholehearted. It is hard for you to separate love and sex, and even your most erotic impulses and fantasies are typically driven by deep affection for your mate. Drawn to colorful, interesting people, you thrive in a love relationship that has an epic feel, as if you and your significant other are the stars of your own romantic drama.

Venus in Virgo

Venus in Virgo tends to be sensitive and insecure in love and romance, and this quality of reserved dignity is part of your appeal. Critical of those you care about, you're always trying to help them better themselves. You're a great listener and you keenly observe potential suitors in hopes of learning what makes them tick. You may not show a lot of emotion outwardly, but are extremely sensitive to what others think of you. More than anything, you need to feel needed and appreciated and would rather be alone than with someone who fails to measure up to your high standards.

Although you're capable of complete involvement, you prefer privacy and shy away from demonstrative displays of affection. The perfectionist in you longs for a lover you can place on a pedestal and worship from afar. However, your earthy, practical side wants a loving relationship that functions orderly and efficiently. In the bedroom, you're endearingly modest, but are responsive to touch and over time you reveal the deeper layers of your innate sensuality.

Venus in Libra

This gracious, peace-loving sign is invariably polite, considerate, and aware of what other people are feeling. An aesthetic as well as a romantic, you enjoy being surrounded by beauty and thrive in a committed, loving partnership. Civilized and refined, you're upset by bad manners and avoid discord of any kind. Since a serene relationship is so important to you, you'll make just about any sacrifice for the sake of peace and harmony. You become quietly resentful if you feel that you're being taken advantage of, although you make it easy for more aggressive people to bully you.

In Libra, Venus is at her most seductive. However, your seductiveness is subtle and manifests itself in ways that are neither vulgar nor overtly sexual. In the bedroom, you're gifted at creating a romantic setting, and enhancing the mood with scented candles, soft music, and silky sheets. Moreover, you are totally devoted to your partner's needs and committed to fulfilling his or her every wish and desire.

Venus in Scorpio

Venus in Scorpio confers magnetic intensity and a deeply emotional, romantic, and sexual nature. An extremist in life and in love, you give yourself totally to everything you do, and expect the same kind of involvement in return. While part of your appeal lies in your apparent obsession with the object of your affection, what you actually have is a strong, jealous need to control your significant other. However, this may not be immediately apparent, and you'll probably never admit to it. You not only possess your beloved, but somehow you make it seem attractive to be possessed.

When first meeting people, you're likely to be cautious, taking time to observe them. You're able to bide your time and wait for the right moment to take the relationship further. There's a hint of danger with you, which can be a major turn on for some people and your actions promise deep commitment and intense sexual pleasure. Your tendency to guard your privacy can make you seem like a tantalizing mystery just waiting to be investigated.

Venus in Sagittarius

Those with Venus in Sagittarius have a carefree attitude toward love and relationships. You're upbeat and easy to like, but not particularly dependable where your affections are concerned. When you find someone you really like, you don't hold back, and it's never hard to figure out exactly where you stand on emotional issues. Attracted to easygoing, open-minded people who share your lust for life, you turn them on with your jokes, grand schemes, and friendly, flirtatious behavior. You won't put up with a boring lover for long; if things get really tedious, you may experience an overwhelming desire to run away. Usually this means that you need to get out and experience something new and interesting before returning home reinvigorated. Curious about all things sexual, you'll play the field for as long as possible as part of your overall quest for life experience.

Venus in Capricorn

Venusian goats are proud, dependable, loyal, careful, and controlled. Your romantic feelings can be very strong on the inside, yet outwardly you respond with reserve and caution when it comes to expressing your emotions. Traditional, practical, and cautious, you rarely let your heart rule your head and, since you're not likely to fall head-over-heels, your approach to a long-term union is more pragmatic than sentimental. However, what you lack in sweet-talk, you make up for in loyalty and fidelity. Duty-conscious and reliable, you don't shirk your responsibilities, and you show your love by taking care of your loved ones.

You project an aura of competency, and your cool-headed behavior is extremely attractive. You admire hard-working, resourceful people like yourself, and you want a life partner you can count on and be proud of. It certainly doesn't hurt if he or she is good-looking, prosperous, and accomplished. You're a realist, so you're not expecting perfection, just someone who is perfect for you. Moreover, you're willing to wait for as long as it takes to find your Mr. or Ms. Right.

Venus in Aquarius

Essentially an intellectual, you live more in your mind than in your body. Yet despite your open, friendly manner, you somehow come off as cool and detached. Your freewheeling attitude concerning standards of behavior is unusual to the point of eccentricity and you set your own rules. Since your head is usually somewhere in the clouds, you're often oblivious to the fact that someone is attracted to you. You get noticed because you're offbeat and original and people respect the way you champion the underdog, even when it puts you in the line of fire.

Friendship, rather than sex or romance, is at the foundation of your intimate relationships and there's a good chance that you'll become involved with a broad spectrum of people during your lifetime. In a relationship, you're looking for intellectual rapport, and are attracted to individuals who are quirky in their own right. It's easy for others to be with you because you don't make emotional demands and your attitude lends your romantic alliances a feeling of freedom and respect.

Venus in Pisces

Venus in Pisces is sensitive, dreamy, and sentimental. Naturally kind and unselfish, you give whatever you deem necessary to help others, but some may take advantage of you. A highly dependent person, who spends a lot of time falling in and out of love, you're very much in need of a nurturing partner. With your warm, gracious manner, you have little trouble establishing close relationships, but your strong emotions and vivid imagination sometimes cloud your judgment. What you're seeking is an otherworldly romance that's exceedingly difficult to find on the material plane.

There's something mystical and ethereal in you that appeals to others on a deep level. You exude grace and charm, and your imagination makes you a fascinating conversationalist. You prefer to wait for the other person to make the first move, so your ideal lover is the one who takes the initiative. But, when things don't go well for you in a relationship, your extreme sensitivity can leave you open to hurt feelings; at times you push this martyred attitude a bit too far.

6

Moon/Venus Combinations

THE MOON IN YOUR HOROSCOPE SYMBOLIZES YOUR EMOTIONAL REACTIONS, and has to do with your responses to love and affection. Its sign in the birth chart indicates the ways you're likely to react in an intimate union. Venus, the embodiment of romantic love and physical attraction, indicates your "love quotient"—your attitude toward close relationships, how you express (or repress) your romantic feelings, what you are seeking from a partner, and what you expect to give in return.

The combination of the signs of the Moon and Venus reveals your emotional strengths and insecurities, the role love plays in your life, how you go about attracting a lover, and how you're likely to behave within the context of a romantic relationship. The emotional characteristics of the signs differ greatly. By understanding the astrological dynamics of your own Moon/Venus combination, or that of your partner or potential lover, you gain tremendous insight into another of the basic motivating forces of life—the love nature.

Combinations of the Moon in Aries

Moon in Aries/Venus in Aries

With both the Moon and Venus in fiery Aries, you are spontaneity personified. Your affection is easily ignited, and you're inclined to follow your heart and impulses no matter where they lead. However, your passion and enthusiasm are likely to die a swift death unless your partner is capable of fanning the flames with exciting new thrills. You dislike routine; challenges and adventure turn you on. You have a fun-loving, daring nature, and like being with a romantic partner who is a playmate as well as a lover.

Moon in Aries/Venus in Taurus

With the directness of Aries, and the patience, focus, and determination of Taurus, your approach to love is straightforward and uncomplicated. When you want something bad enough, you refuse to take "no" for an answer and pursue the object of your affection with dogged persistence. A dynamic lover, your irresistible mix of bold aggression and languid sensuality rarely fails to attract potential partners. However, while many are called, few are chosen. Your heart has more patience then your libido, and prefers to wait for true love.

Moon in Aries/Venus in Gemini

With this combination, your playful, outgoing personality brings many romantic opportunities. However, you're notoriously difficult to pin down, and your restless nature keeps you from sticking with one person for long. You're not unreliable; you just find boredom absolutely insufferable. A delightful, fun-loving lover yourself, you'll stay around as long as your partner offers stimulation and excitement.

Moon in Aries/Venus in Cancer

You long to be independent and unfettered, but often find yourself attending to the needs of others. You're serious and humorous by turns, and your ideal mate is intuitive enough to sense your emotional rhythms. Sometimes it's frustrating for you, because you generally know what others are feeling, but no one seems to understand your moods. In the bedroom, however, you combine the best aspects of sensuality, tenderness, and excitement to be a truly awesome lover.

Moon in Aries/Venus in Leo

Aries' impulsive approach to romance is complemented by Leo's regal confidence. As long as a potential partner sends admiring glances in your direction, you pursue your goal with passion and vigor. It never even dawns on you that the other person may not be interested. You expect everyone to want to be with you and—with your sparkling personality and enthusiasm—most do. In bed, you're a fiery lover and hearts and flowers are rarely as appealing to you as drama, fun, and excitement.

Moon in Aries/Venus in Virgo

Neither flamboyant, nor stodgy, you enjoy good times that are tasteful and refined as well as exciting and adventurous. When you work, you work hard, but when you play you just want to put aside your other concerns and have some fun. At times you may seem headstrong, because you're convinced that your way of doing things is best. You'd rather be alone than with someone who doesn't live up to your high standards.

Moon in Aries/Venus in Libra

Despite your need to choose between independence and partnership, romantic relationships are central to your life. You love the rituals of courtship so much that if the spark goes out of your romance you immediately begin looking around for new thrills. Your approach to lovemaking is full of delightful contradictions. Aries prefers to charge right in, but Libra hesitates. Your ideal mate understands your enigmatic nature, and is capable of switching gears to match your pace and rhythm.

Moon in Aries/Venus in Scorpio

Falling in love sends you into a state of bliss, but Aries' restless heart keeps you on the move. Scorpio makes you deeply passionate, and your libido generally leads the way. When you see someone you want, you set your sights on that person with unremitting zeal. In relationships, you're either blazing hot or icy cold, never lukewarm. As far as you are concerned, love—and life—has to be all or nothing.

Moon in Aries/Venus in Sagittarius

You prefer being footloose and fancy free to settling down with one person. Consequently, long-term unions are not your strong suit. While one of the warmest, friendliest people around, you're just not particularly emotional or relationship-oriented. You're not exactly interested in forever, and no one makes a more exciting and carefree lover than you.

Moon in Aries/Venus in Capricorn

Outwardly controlled, your lusty libido swiftly surfaces behind closed doors. Once you let go, you come on strong—and have the sexual prowess to back it up. You'd much rather *do* something, than sit around and talk about love. Passionate and romantic, you can also be demanding and moody, which can make you difficult to live with. Due to your high standards, you tend to get irritable when things don't go as you think they should.

Moon in Aries/Venus in Aquarius

For you, life is an adventure, and you love to walk on the wild side. Whether a friend or a lover, you're never boring. You eagerly embrace new experiences, and your continuing quest for excitement prompts you to change partners frequently. Because you need change and stimulation, a quiet, harmonious relationship drives you crazy. You like to have time to explore your own interests, so your ideal partner is the person who doesn't expect you to be joined at the hip.

Moon in Aries/Venus in Pisces

You fall in love with your entire being, and you feel as if no one has ever loved as you do. Charming, impulsive, and impractical, you're also totally irresistible. You project an air of glamorous excitement that has been known to sweep potential suitors right off their feet. Beneath your easygoing public exterior, there is an adventurous, bawdy nature best expressed in private. Consequently, you can get involved in some pretty tempestuous romances.

Combinations of the Moon in Taurus

Moon in Taurus/Venus in Aries

You have a zest for all the good things in life—including love. When you find someone you like, you jump right in with a compelling mix of aggressiveness and sensuality. Easygoing and upbeat, you find it hard to understand why other people go through so many ups and downs in their relationships. While closeness and stability in a union are important, your need to be your own person takes precedence. As long as your partner allows you some breathing room, you don't let too many things bother you.

Moon in Taurus/Venus in Taurus

An exceedingly tactile person, all types of physical contact appeal to you—long hugs, lingering kisses, and sensual massages with oils and scented lotions. On one hand, you are loving and romantic, but you're also sensible and practical. Ultimately, security and stability matter more to you than thrills and excitement. Moreover, your tastes in love and sex are straightforward; you don't need a lot of frills to entice you.

Moon in Taurus/Venus in Gemini

Part of you wants to be free and unencumbered, but you also long to settle down with a mate who understands your inner conflicts. A great deal of your energy is channeled into verbal communication—and one of your favorite topics of conversation is sex. In fact, you enjoy sexual banter almost as much as making love. You particularly get off on discussing what you're going to do with your lover once talk turns into action.

Moon in Taurus/Venus in Cancer

For you, security is all-important and casual love affairs have no place in your plans. Once you make a commitment, your mate can rely on you to be there through thick and thin. Good food and great sex are at the heart of your approach to love. You're at your best sharing a fabulous meal with your lover—and then adjourning to the bedroom for some world-class cuddling.

Moon in Taurus/Venus in Leo

You enjoy feeling like an honored luminary, and particularly like being appreciated for your generosity and prowess in the bedroom. Taurus makes you meticulous and unhurried in everything you do, while Leo adds the desire to amaze your partner with your sexual abilities. Your ideal mate values your passionate sensuality, and is willing to overlook your bouts of stubbornness and determination to have things your own way.

Moon in Taurus/Venus in Virgo

A down-to-earth individual, you're painstakingly careful about everything you do and have a refined appreciation for the small things in life. Where love and romance are concerned, you're caring, modest, affectionate, and thoughtful. Aware that actions speak louder than words, you show your love in tangible ways—and your consideration and sensuality make you an exceptional lover. All you really want is to live a full and useful life, with your true love by your side to enjoy it with you.

Moon in Taurus/Venus in Libra

At once an idealist and a hedonist, romance and sex are intertwined in your mind. In youth, starry-eyed sentimentality may propel you into various romantic escapades, but once you find your soul mate you're a devoted and steadfast partner. In the bedroom, your gift for using both words and touch to engage your lover leads to extraordinarily sensual, exciting lovemaking.

Moon in Taurus/Venus in Scorpio

While your sexual magnetism attracts many potential suitors, your steamy nature is most likely to find expression in a long-lasting intimate union. Your smoldering sexuality and penetrating gaze has a mesmerizing effect on those around you—and you use it to ignite the fires of love. For you, sex is more than a mere physical act, it's a transcendent merging of two souls. Consequently, one-night stands and casual affairs hold little attraction for you.

Moon in Taurus/Venus in Sagittarius

While sex is fun and games for Venus in Sagittarius, your Moon in Taurus impels you to seek the stability of a close relationship. As a result, you sometimes feel as if you're being pulled in opposite directions where your love life is concerned. Passionate in bed, you could burn out a lover with your enthusiasms. Your ideal mate shares your lust for life and love, and appreciates your willingness to explore new and novel ways to enhance your mutual pleasure between the sheets.

Moon in Taurus/Venus in Capricorn

Stiff and formal in the presence of company, in the privacy of your own bedroom you're an exceptionally sensual, relaxed bedmate. You like to take your time, making sure that both you and your partner enjoy every delightful moment between the sheets. A traditionalist, you actively seek out the white picket fence lifestyle that more unconventional types seem to avoid like the plague. In love, you tend to be careful initially, but once you find the right person you're more than happy to settle down to a long-term union.

Moon in Taurus/Venus in Aquarius

With both the Moon and Venus in Fixed signs, you can be stubborn and set in your ways. Yet you're also prone to Aquarius's occasional spurts of unconventionality. While one part of your head is mired in traditional values, another is rebellious and eccentric. Outgoing and sociable, you enjoy parties and going out with friends. Since you tend to be emotionally elusive, intimate relationships can be difficult for you to sustain. However, when it comes to sex, you're open-minded and willing to explore all sorts of erotic pleasures.

Moon in Taurus/Venus in Pisces

You have a rare ability to combine the romantic with the practical, the earthy with the spiritual. You're idealistic, and casual romance has no place in your life. When you love someone, both your body and your soul get into the act; physical love alone just doesn't do it for you. In bed, you like to take your time exploring all the possibilities of sensual pleasure.

Combinations of the Moon in Gemini

Moon in Gemini/Venus in Aries

A delightful, fun-loving companion, you can't help attracting friends and admirers. You exude the kind of sex appeal that promises sensual magic, and you deliver on your promises. Your approach to love is super enthusiastic and, when you see someone you like, you don't worry about the consequences. Fidelity is not your strong suit, and you fall in and out of love easily. You cherish your independence and, with your mercurial nature, rarely stay put long enough for anyone to pin you down.

Moon in Gemini/Venus in Taurus

You are among the most sensual of the Moon in Gemini lovers. Your approach to love and sex is cool and clearheaded, but your deep-seated appreciation for the joys of the flesh makes you a desirable lover. For you, lovemaking is both a physical and mental experience and you make sure neither side is shortchanged. You get off on sharing thoughts and ideas with your partner—especially in the bedroom. Moreover, you're particularly adept at expressing your sexuality in word as well as deed.

Moon in Gemini/Venus in Gemini

In bed and out you are creative, lively, full of wild ideas, and willing to try just about anything at least once. Communication is important to you and you want a lover who is also a friend and confidant. As far as you're concerned, no amount of physical attraction makes up for a lack of shared interests or an inability to talk with your bed partner. Always eager for fresh experiences, when love throws you for a loop, you get back up on your horse and ride off again in search of a new romance.

Moon in Gemini/Venus in Cancer

Your heart and mind both crave the fulfillment of a loving relationship, but you often have great difficulty expressing your deepest feelings. In bed and elsewhere, you just want to have a good time. With your playful personality, you enjoy sharing laughter and jokes in between all the kissing and cuddling. At times you may resort to cleverness, witty remarks, and good-natured teasing to keep your partner at arm's length emotionally.

Moon in Gemini/Venus in Leo

The image you project is magnetic and exciting, and you're never dull or boring. You enjoy the drama of being in love, and making a big show of courtship and romance. Although you intend to be faithful when seriously involved, you just can't help being curious and honestly interested in all kinds of people. Your ideal mate knows how to keep rekindling the initial spark to maintain the feeling of newness between you.

Moon in Gemini /Venus in Virgo

Naturally sociable and friendly, you like people and enjoy exchanging ideas with everyone you meet. Bright, lively, witty conversations stimulate you almost as much as sexual encounters—and the lover who makes you laugh will steal your heart. You need a partner who is your intellectual equal and challenges you mentally; you'd rather be single than stuck in a relationship with someone who isn't clever enough to hold your interest.

Moon in Gemini/Venus in Libra

With this highly intellectual combination, you prefer keeping things light and unemotional—even in your most intimate moments. Words are your forte, and language is your most powerful tool of seduction. You enjoy bantering with your significant other and love to keep in touch even when you can't be together physically. In the bedroom, you're an inventive, romantic lover. Beauty and comfort gratify your refined sensibilities, and tasteful décor adds to your sensual pleasure.

Moon in Gemini/Venus in Scorpio

You are passionate and demanding in intimate relationships. While one part of you longs for an intensely ardent, long-term relationship, the other part prefers skimming happily along the surface of love without taking the ultimate plunge. In bed, you project a sultry seductiveness that sets your partner's mind and body afire. In social situations, your incisive wit and provocative gaze provide you with many opportunities for casual—and not so casual—flirtation.

Moon in Gemini/Venus in Sagittarius

Love is mainly fun and games for those with this happy-go-lucky combination and romance works best for you when it's rooted in intellectual rapport. While open to the joys engendered by sexual desire, you refuse to let a close relationship slow you down. For you, sensual pleasure is only one of the ways to enjoy life, and you're eager to experience them all. As far as you're concerned, there is too much to see and do to get bogged down in one place, or with one person.

Moon in Gemini/Venus in Capricorn

Although you want a romantic alliance that allows you a certain measure of freedom, you demand a strong commitment and total loyalty from your mate. You're changeable and emotionally contradictory, and your volatility is puzzling to your significant other. You may be flirty and playful one moment, utterly serious the next. Nevertheless, you exhibit your strong libido in the privacy of the bedroom. With your ideal partner at your side, your reserve swiftly departs and you enjoy experimenting with new sexual positions and toys.

Moon in Gemini/Venus in Aquarius

In social situations your wit, charm, and flirtatious manner attract people and make them want to get to know you better. In an intimate relationship you can take or leave romance, but intellectual companionship and a partner who shares your interests are a must. In the privacy of the boudoir, you're open-minded and will try almost anything—at least once. Sensual enhancements such as sex toys keep you interested and add variety and spice to your lovemaking.

Moon in Gemini/Venus in Pisces

Although you want the grounding of a stable, long-term partnership, you're fearful of losing your independence. Sociable, chatty, vibrant Gemini wants friendship, conversation, and constant intellectual stimulation, while the idealistic fish craves moonlight, poetry, and romance. As a result, you're almost as happy when thinking and talking about romance, as when you're actually engaging in sex. Bewitched by imagination and dreams, you particularly enjoy acting out your erotic fantasies with your lover.

Combinations of the Moon in Cancer

Moon in Cancer/Venus in Aries

The impetuous exuberance of Aries is continually at odds with the moody apprehension engendered by Cancer. Since your pride is easily wounded, you're subject to fits of depression when your actions are challenged. Your subtle charm gives you your smoldering charisma, but insecurity keeps you from making bold moves unless you're sure they'll be welcomed. You shine in the bedroom, where you combine tenderness and consideration with breathtaking sexual innovation.

Moon in Cancer/Venus in Taurus

You don't take love lightly and when you commit to someone you do so with your whole heart. Comfort, stability, and security matter most to you in an intimate union and when you find Mr. or Ms. Right you have little hesitation about settling down to an idyllic life together. In a close relationship, you're extremely loyal and responsive to your lover's needs and desires. More than anything, you appreciate sensory delights, and are happiest when you can combine two or more—such as good food or drink with great sex.

Moon in Cancer/Venus in Gemini

The sensitive, imaginative, intuitive crab experiences the world through feelings and emotions, whereas the rational twins focus mainly on words and ideas. This dichotomy makes you a fascinating, dynamic, multifaceted—if somewhat difficult to understand—romantic partner. With the two sides of your character working in sync, you dazzle your bedmate with a unique mix of witty sexual banter and heightened sensuality. Although your lover may tire of dealing with your shifting moods, he or she will certainly never be bored.

Moon in Cancer/Venus in Cancer

People with both the Moon and Venus in Cancer are thoughtful and generous with those they love, but are also extremely sensitive and self-protective. In the bedroom, you want lots of affection and romance; hugging, kissing, touching, and other preliminaries are important to you. Yet, despite your strongly sensual nature, you only feel satisfied with a partner you truly care about. When you're in a secure and stable intimate relationship, you can't do enough for your mate.

Moon in Cancer/Venus in Leo

Genuinely romantic and strongly protective of your beloved, you thrive on intimacy and the blissful feeling of being part of a couple. You long to be cherished and adored, and are at your best when you receive the love and devotion you crave. You're the most thoughtful of lovers and you consider your partner's satisfaction between the sheets to be as important as your own.

Moon in Cancer/Venus in Virgo

Nothing makes you happier than taking care of your loved ones, but you sometimes come across as overprotective or smothering. Sensitive and passive, you're often tempted to just stand aside and let your mate call all the shots. Because you're so nurturing and giving, people may take advantage of you—never realizing that you're longing to be catered to and fussed over for a change.

Moon in Cancer/Venus in Libra

The refined, sensitive, partnership-oriented individuals born under this combination can barely wait to settle down to a lifetime of wedded bliss, and you do everything possible to make your relationship conform to your idea of what true love ought to be. All you really want is to make your partner happy, but your determination to place him or her at the center of your world may be misinterpreted as smothering. In the bedroom, luxurious surroundings and a beautiful romantic setting heighten your sexual desires.

Moon in Cancer/Venus in Scorpio

In a romantic union, you're passionate, intense, demanding, intuitive, and self-protective. You crave love, but—easily hurt—are fearful of exposing your emotional vulnerability to another person. When happy, no one is nicer or more generous, but when upset, you retreat to a corner to brood.

In the bedroom, your keen intuition helps you tap into your mate's deepest desires, and you delight your lover with sensual erotic lovemaking.

Moon in Cancer/Venus in Sagittarius

You go back and forth between wanting a secure home life and longing for the independence to roam the world. You also have a thirst for adventure and your threshold for boredom is extremely low. Until you come to terms with the diverse sides of your nature, it's hard to find the love you seek, but when you reconcile your conflicting impulses, you're a loyal and caring partner. Once assured of your partner's affection, your amazing sexual prowess and uninhibited sensuality keep your lover enthralled.

Moon in Cancer/Venus in Capricorn

Dignified and reserved, you're unlikely to gush or be unduly demonstrative in public. You thrive on domesticity, and probably want a traditional marriage and family life. A genuine romantic, you like to touch, hug, kiss, and cuddle your significant other, and surprise him or her with sentimental gifts. Beneath the covers, your tenderness and sensuality reveal an emotional sensitivity that you keep well guarded outside the bedroom.

Moon in Cancer/Venus in Aquarius

The conservative crab is basically domestic and longs to settle down, but the rebellious water bearer is freedom-loving and individualistic. The suitor who is willing to make allowances for your mood swings is the one most likely to win your affections. Playfully innovative in the bedroom, you're both fun-loving and romantic between the sheets. In a loving union, you'll willingly make room for a little experimentation in your sex life.

Moon in Cancer/Venus in Pisces

In matters of the heart, you're a consummate romantic. You're always in love, searching for love, or involved in a rich fantasy life where love rules. You thrive when everything is going well, but feel completely shattered if your relationship fails to live up to your expectations. The traditional trappings of courtship and romance inflame your imagination and stir your passion. The suitor who provides a sumptuous setting, with music and scented candles for an evening of amorous lovemaking, is the one most likely to win your favor.

Combinations of the Moon in Leo

Moon in Leo/Venus in Aries

These impulsive individuals are big risk takers. You love people, and they're drawn to you. Colorful, dramatic, slightly outrageous personalities appeal to your theatrical nature, and in your love life, you'll probably experience a few hard tumbles before settling down. Although your pride is wounded when things go awry, you rebound from love's trials with remarkable ease. While you always expect to be the center of attention, in bed you're generous and considerate of your mate's wishes.

Moon in Leo/Venus in Taurus

Lunar lions with Venus in Taurus really know how to live and love. "Only the best of everything," may well be your motto. Lavish in your affections and generous with material things, you're willing to give your all to your lover—but you expect the same kind of devotion in return. In the bedroom, you enjoy luxuriating in long, lazy sessions of erotic lovemaking. Few bed partners have your stamina between the sheets, and your moments of intimacy virtually crackle with intensity.

Moon in Leo/Venus in Gemini

Yours is a gregarious, outgoing nature. Eager to be the center of attention, you're a riveting storyteller and unabashed flirt, with a decided knack for keeping an audience, or a single listener, totally enthralled. Your ideal life partner has many interesting aspects for you to discover, and doesn't mind sharing you with your various creative pursuits. Your way with words extends to your most intimate moments, and you enjoy exchanging lusty banter with your partner before, during, and after lovemaking.

Moon in Leo/Venus in Cancer

Exuberant and outgoing in company, you can be shy in intimate situations. You prefer keeping your true emotions hidden until you're sure your prospective partner shares your feelings. Once involved, you make a generous, romantic, and strongly protective lover. In the bedroom, you combine the best of intuition and sensitivity with amazing sexual prowess. Since pleasing your mate is a point of pride, you make sure that he or she feels loved and appreciated.

Moon in Leo/Venus in Leo

For you, love is a many-splendored experience, and you're happiest when playing the starring role in the drama of your own love life. You enjoy making a production of lovemaking—the bigger and more theatrical the better. Sumptuous bedroom settings and erotic attire get your sexual juices flowing. However, sometimes you get so caught up in the glamour of love and romance that you forget about the everyday details that make up a close relationship.

Moon in Leo/Venus in Virgo

In a close relationship, you're ardent and affectionate, and romance and intellectual rapport matter a lot to you. In most areas of your life, you're optimistic and confident, but in an intimate union, you tend to be cautious and analytical. Your shyness in love stems from a deep-seated fear that your partner may judge you or be critical of your actions. An idealist, you want a lover who meets your expectations, yet you resent being held to the same high standard in return.

Moon in Leo/Venus in Libra

You crave the attention and approval of others, and your sociability and sunny disposition assure your popularity. With romance as a priority in your life, you invest energy in making yourself appealing to potential suitors and rarely have to look for love, because it finds you. You are (or pretend to be) a bit shy about sex and enjoy being coaxed, cajoled, and courted. You dislike spending time alone, and your desire for companionship is as strong as your need for affection. Although friendly to everyone, you prefer the company of attractive, cultured, mentally stimulating individuals who share your interests.

Moon in Leo/Venus in Scorpio

You have an intensely sensual nature and an all-or-nothing approach to love that fascinates potential suitors. In a close relationship you have a great deal to give, but demand so much in return that your partner may find your expectations a bit overwhelming. The physical side of love is important to you, and you enjoy making a big production out of your most intimate moments. There is nothing passive about your temperament, and fiery lover's quarrels followed by passionate reconciliations may be part of your normal routine.

Moon in Leo/Venus in Sagittarius

In a love union, you're passionate, generous, and magnanimous. Playfulness and exuberance define your personality, and you attract plenty of companions willing to join in the fun and games. You shine at parties and other social occasions, especially if you are the guest of honor. Your sexual expression evolves naturally from your unending zest for living and you're a lot of fun between the sheets. If you sometimes seem nonchalant about lovemaking, it's simply a reflection of your open-minded, free-spirited attitude toward relationships.

Moon in Leo/Venus in Capricorn

Your proud nature and fragile ego require constant reassurance in the form of admiration and appreciation. Despite your lusty libido, you bring caution and practicality to the mating dance. However, once you're sure you're with the right person, you're anything but shy. Endurance is your forte, and your stamina in the bedroom virtually guarantees your lover's satisfaction.

Moon in Leo/Venus in Aquarius

Lively social occasions are the perfect stage for your sparkling wit and riveting stories, and your gregarious personality lures an eclectic mix of suitors to your side. Drawn to original thinkers and creative free spirits, you'll soon lose interest in a partner with whom you have no intellectual connection. Emotionally, you may be somewhat cool and detached, but there is nothing cool about your smoldering sexuality. In the bedroom, you're generous and anxious to please.

Moon in Leo/Venus in Pisces

You project a magic allure that draws love into your life, and it's a good thing because you regard love as vital to your happiness. When everything goes well, you're on top of the world, but if a love affair turns sour you're totally devastated. You dream big, and you enjoy acting out your desires in the bedroom. Setting the stage with luxurious things provides the proper backdrop for your highly sensuous, romantic lovemaking.

Combinations of the Moon in Virgo

Moon in Virgo/Venus in Aries

Innately sympathetic and nurturing, your genuine interest in other people's problems prompts you to offer help whenever possible. Even so, your help rarely comes without strings and, since your own ego is quite fragile, you're actually more adept at dishing out criticism than accepting it. However, in the throes of passion, Virgo's cool reserve and desire for perfection melts under Aries' sizzling intensity.

Moon in Virgo/Venus in Taurus

Initially cautious, you prefer building a sexual relationship on a strong, solid foundation; one-night stands have no place in your love life. Once you find a compatible mate, you're loyal and dependable, but also sexy and extremely sensual. Your approach to sex is uncomplicated and direct. Tactile by nature, you communicate with your lover through touch as well as words. A beautifully appointed room, with fresh flowers and candlelight puts you in the mood for love.

Moon in Virgo/Venus in Gemini

Your curiosity and diversity of interests brings you into contact with all types of people, yet you manage to steer clear of empty glamour and promises. Mr. or Ms. Right holds your interest and attention by dazzling you with wit, charm, and bright ideas, while creating a bond built on sincerity and mutual respect. You will go to a lot of trouble to please your bed partner, as long as things don't get too emotionally intense or demanding.

Moon in Virgo/Venus in Cancer

Taking care of others is your forte, and you're the ultimate helpful, giving partner. You enjoy doing things for your beloved, and will work hard to make his or her life easier and more pleasurable. In the bedroom, you want more from sex than just physical release. You need love, understanding, and emotional security as well. Sensitive and naturally passive, you can fall into the habit of letting your significant other call all the shots. Then, if things don't turn out the way you hoped, you feel let down and blame your mate for your disappointment.

Moon in Virgo/Venus in Leo

In matters of the heart, you're warm and passionate, but your desire for perfection undermines your intimate relationships. You're continually searching for the ultimate erotic experience. Extremely sensitive, you never mean to hurt your partner's feelings, but Moon in Virgo's habit of nitpicking could drive anyone straight up a wall. When you get the attention, appreciation, and physical satisfaction you desire, you're likely to be much happier and less inclined to find fault with your significant other.

Moon in Virgo/Venus in Virgo

Sensitive and kindhearted, you can also be cool and dispassionate. Little is left to chance in your love life, as you plan all the details of a romantic encounter in advance. Naturally sentimental, yet apprehensive about expressing your true feelings, you prefer demonstrating affection though thoughtfulness and consideration rather than with words of love. While your hidden passions can be stirred by a persistent suitor, it generally takes time for you to reveal your deepest desires.

Moon in Virgo/Venus in Libra

While love is important to you, you rarely lead with your heart. Although your sex drive and staying power in the bedroom are quite impressive, your sensitive nature and refined sensibilities are easily upset by too much physical or emotional intensity. Consequently, you prefer keeping your love life on an even keel. A neat, orderly, harmonious union is more appealing to you than one that is wildly passionate and emotionally chaotic. Your ideal mate is as attractive, good mannered, charming, and well turned out as you.

Moon in Virgo/Venus in Scorpio

In love and life, you play your cards close to the chest. You don't grant many people access to your inner sanctum, but make a thoughtful and devoted friend or lover. Although you can be critical of your partner, you're exceedingly loyal and, behind closed doors, you're a passionate and romantic bedmate. A master of detail, little if anything escapes your notice; you pay careful attention to your mate's likes and dislikes and then do your best to accommodate them.

Moon in Virgo/Venus in Sagittarius

You are romantic and warmhearted, but also critical of anyone who doesn't measure up to your high standards. Your Venusian archer craves excitement, variety, and independence, but the lunar virgin prefers the emotional security of a permanent union. Your fiery sensuality simmers just below the surface, and sexy banter liberates your quick wit and playful sense of humor. Spending time outdoors with your significant other sparks your libido, and provides a natural backdrop for your amorous lovemaking.

Moon in Virgo/Venus in Capricorn

Reserved and slow to warm up in public, with a patient, loving partner you're affectionate and caring. In the welcoming comfort of hearth and home, where your surroundings reflect your affinity for classic style and tradition, your erotic sensibilities erupt with abandon. A very sensual lover, you're unable to resist anything that makes your body feel good. Even so, you want nothing less than a secure, long-term romantic union, and casual suitors with empty promises are swiftly shown the door.

Moon in Virgo/Venus in Aquarius

Despite your air of aloof detachment, you're more in need of affection and companionship than you're willing to let on. You're actually as self-sufficient and independent as you appear, but also like coming home to the comfort and security of a committed relationship. You absorb new ideas with a ravenous hunger, and your first connection with a potential suitor is likely to be mental. There is an intellectual quality to your sexuality as well, and the intelligent, witty lover who makes your head spin with innovative ideas—in bed and out—is the one most likely to catch and hold your interest.

Moon in Virgo/Venus in Pisces

Those born under Venus in Pisces are romantic, sensitive, and sentimental, and place a high priority on the importance of a loving relationship in their lives. However, Moon in Virgo craves companionship of a thoughtful, intellectual variety. While the dreamy part of your nature casts an invisible web of seduction around a potential suitor, your own two feet are planted firmly on the ground. Although your ultimate desire may be to merge sexual pleasure with spiritual union, you need to know that there is an earthy, practical side to your life together as well.

Combinations of the Moon in Libra

Moon in Libra/Venus in Aries

The romantic charms of your Moon in Libra are enhanced by the strong sensuality of Venus in Aries, making you an alluring, enthusiastic, and passionate lover. You often find yourself trying to choose between independence and the comfortable feeling of being half a couple. Initially, love may be little more than a game to you, during which you flirt with playful abandon. However, eventually you'll feel compelled to settle down to a pleasant long-term union. Once involved, you'll throw yourself into the task of creating a charming, balanced atmosphere with graceful, harmonious surroundings where love can thrive.

Moon in Libra/Venus in Taurus

A genuine romantic, nothing makes you happier than being alone with your partner in a paradise of your own making. The idealistic Moon in Libra in you craves a lover you can put on a pedestal and worship. However, earthy, sensual Venus in Taurus wants a real life mate to share your most intimate moments. In the bedroom, you respond most readily to an elegant style of lovemaking that builds slowly toward the peak of desire.

Moon in Libra/Venus in Gemini

More intellectual than physical or emotional, it is not unusual for you to find a spirited discussion as stimulating as a passionate sexual encounter. In the bedroom, your relaxed, easygoing nature makes you an ideal bedmate, likely to go along with whatever your partner wants. An incurable romantic, you're prone to falling in love with the idea of love. However, you're easily bored and may go through several romances before settling down. The charismatic lover with the wit and intelligence to keep you interested is the one most likely to catch and keep you.

Moon in Libra/Venus in Cancer

Although you may act as if romance is all fun and games, in matters of the heart you play for keeps. You crave the kind of closeness that includes total cooperation. When things don't go as you'd hoped, you may feel resentful, but rarely allow your anger to show. Instead you bury your disappointment, and try harder to achieve a happy union. Your ideal lover intuits your moods and his or her patience and tenderness unlocks your deeper passions in the bedroom.

Moon in Libra/Venus in Leo

The romantic, idealistic individuals with this combination expect so much from an intimate relationship that the reality rarely lives up to the dream. Yet you probably won't feel fulfilled without someone special to share your life. Generous with your love and affection, you shower your partner with loving words and gestures. In bed and out, you crave constant attention, romance, appreciation, and love. If you get what you want, there is no more passionate and considerate lover than you. Sociable and outgoing yourself, you need a significant other who also enjoys going places, meeting people, and doing all kinds of interesting things.

Moon in Libra/Venus in Virgo

A perfectionist in love and in life, you're not likely to settle for less than the best just because you dislike being alone. Even after you find your ideal mate, you'll probably continue to notice his or her flaws and try to fix them. Emotionally, you're rather high maintenance, but no one makes a more doting or helpful companion than you. In or out of the bedroom, you are attentive, loving, and caring. You do all kinds of little things to satisfy your significant other's desires and enhance his or her quality of life.

Moon in Libra/Venus in Libra

Your amiable nature and genial disposition make you particularly easy to get along with. Where love and sex are concerned, you enjoy being an object of desire, and your charismatic allure makes the air around you crackle with erotic excitement. Once you form a romantic alliance with another person, you give it your all. Since you thrive on your significant other's love, affection, and approbation, you are readily influenced by his or her opinions, and ideas. In the bedroom, you're more than happy to comply with all of your lover's wishes and desires.

Moon in Libra/Venus in Scorpio

Those born under this combination are an unusual blend of passion and detachment, secrecy and sociability. The scorpion adds ardor and intensity to Libra's romantic idealism. You long for a permanent union, but need to feel comfortable and in control before you commit yourself. Sometimes you are indecisive about your relationship, other times you're jealous and possessive of your mate. In the bedroom, however, you know what your lover wants, and are more than capable of providing it.

Moon in Libra/Venus in Sagittarius

Warm and sociable, you can be found at the center of any gathering. Relationships matter to you, and your amiable, easygoing nature quickly breaks down barriers to love and friendship. You're looking for fun and good times in your romantic alliances. Heavy emotional scenes aren't your style and the lover who hopes to hold you needs to keep things light and playful. Even so, you want a loving companion to share your life and you'll eventually commit to a long-term union with the right person.

Moon in Libra/Venus in Capricorn

Individuals with this combination are studies in contrast. You are lively and full of fun in intimate company, yet swiftly clam up among strangers. In intimate situations, you're cuddly and affectionate one moment, cool and mysterious the next. Since both your Moon and Venus are in Cardinal signs, you like being the one in control, and may often find yourself involved in power struggles with your partner. Ultimately, it takes more than love to hold on to you, you want a life partner who caters to your physical needs in the bedroom and romances you in style in the rest of the house.

Moon in Libra/Venus in Aquarius

You genuinely love people, yet often fail to communicate on an emotional level because you find strong feelings somewhat embarrassing. Instead, your gregarious intellect reaches out to those around you, and responds to any indication of mental rapport. Where long-term commitments are concerned, Aquarius's need for independence is constantly at odds with Libra's belief that life is incomplete without a partner. Your best romantic relationship may well be one that begins as a friendship, and slowly evolves into a physical bond. Between the sheets, there is a decided uniqueness to your lovemaking; you're creative in bed without ever being vulgar.

Moon in Libra/Venus in Pisces

The kind, gentle, thoughtful souls born under this combination don't like to make waves. Your dreamy, romantic nature compels you to seek your other half, and when you find your soul mate it is easy for you to slip into emotional dependency. Your longing for romance can make you prefer a relationship where moments of enchantment exceed those of physical passion. In an intimate union, you like things to be calm and congenial, and you'll do whatever you think necessary to maintain peace and harmony. You may even prefer clinging to a bad relationship, rather than upsetting the status quo.

Combinations of the Moon in Scorpio

Moon in Scorpio/Venus in Aries

You project a magnetic quality that draws others to you. Whereas Aries is independent, enthusiastic, and easygoing, Scorpio makes you jealous, and your suspicious nature can place a strain on your intimate relationships. As a result, you may sometimes feel as if there are two people inhabiting your body. Nevertheless, this is one of the most passionate of the zodiacal combinations and, when aroused, your lusty libido responds with gusto.

Moon in Scorpio/Venus in Taurus

In intimate relationships you're sexy and sensual, but also demanding. At your best, you're caring, generous, and totally devoted to your beloved, but living with you can be extremely difficult. When the possessiveness of Taurus is provoked by the inherent jealousy of Scorpio, your suspicions and angry accusations can drive even the most understanding partner straight up a wall, or even out the door. However, once your passions are let loose, your hearty sexual appetite and incredible physical stamina keep your lover satisfied and by your side throughout the night.

Moon in Scorpio/Venus in Gemini

A great listener and observer of human nature, and an even better talker, you carefully study a potential partner before making any bold moves. However, once your passions are engaged, you entice your lover with sultry verbal suggestions. Your taste for variety in the bedroom leads you to explore all sorts of erotic activities, and sharing your new discoveries with your bedmate serves as verbal foreplay for a night of intense lovemaking.

Moon in Scorpio/Venus in Cancer

In matters of the heart, almost everything you do or say is a response to what you are feeling rather than what you're thinking. Your romantic nature is sensitive but possessive, and you're simply not interested in meaningless sexual interludes. You would rather wait for a partner who returns your love and devotion in equal measure. You often manage to confound potential suitors with your carefully shrouded passionate intensity. In the bedroom, your sensuality and depth of emotion make even the most casual contact seem breathtakingly erotic.

Moon in Scorpio/Venus in Leo

You're an intense and determined person, and nothing stops you from getting what you want. Moreover, your personality is so magnetic that, once you pick someone out of the crowd, you simply wear down his or her resistance until your desires are met. Of course, you're so sexy that it's a rare individual who fails to respond to your appeal. Once involved, you're sensuous, generous, and giving, and no lover is likely to have cause to complain about your performance between the sheets.

Moon in Scorpio/Venus in Virgo

Discriminating and cautious, you don't give your heart to just anyone. However, once you make a commitment, you stick with it through good times and bad. Your idealism and penchant for perfection make you critical and demanding, but when your demands are met you're quite capable of giving your all for love. In the bedroom, it's important for you to be in a position of power and control. The lover who doesn't challenge your authority wins your undying devotion.

Moon in Scorpio/Venus in Libra

You project an alluring combination of sex and romance that draws suitors to you; your unique blend of hot-blooded passion and cool detachment presents an intriguing challenge to potential partners. However, love is serious business for you, and you don't take relationships lightly. The glamour of courtship intoxicates you, and you're forever conjuring up new ways to add a touch of old-fashioned romance to your ardent lovemaking.

Moon in Scorpio/Venus in Scorpio

You're capable of pledging long-lasting affection, but only to a partner who is willing to play by your rules. You're generous, sympathetic, understanding and exceedingly loyal in love, but absolutely refuse to be subjugated to another person's whims. Although a romantic alliance with you isn't easy, few people are capable of generating the intense passion and emotional excitement that seems to come so naturally to you—especially in the bedroom.

Moon in Scorpio/Venus in Sagittarius

People with this combination in their horoscope charts make ardent, and generous—albeit demanding—lovers. The archer in you can be quite flirtatious, and thrives on change. However, you also possess all the loyalty and devotion of Scorpio. As a result, you may go back and forth between independence and commitment. Although you may try to laugh off your possessiveness, you demand absolute fidelity from your mate. If you don't get it, you could decide to leave.

Moon in Scorpio/Venus in Capricorn

You're not likely to devote much time to an intimate union unless you expect it to last. Playing the field doesn't interest you, and you need a partner who takes love as seriously as you do. Even when you find your soul mate, the intensely private portion of your inner nature makes it difficult for you to reveal your true feelings. Moreover, insecurity or lack of trust could cause you to act in a possessive or controlling manner. However, with your ideal mate, you shed your cautious exterior, and reveal your deeply erotic side.

Moon in Scorpio/Venus in Aquarius

The intensity of Scorpio's all-or-nothing approach to intimate relationships doesn't mesh well with Aquarius' easygoing, relaxed attitude toward love and sexuality. Although a cool detachment may pervade your initial approach to romance, the intense emotions smoldering just beneath the surface won't lie dormant for long. Once your spontaneity finds roots in a loving, trusting romantic union, your red-hot libido prompts you to take the lead in imaginative, exciting lovemaking.

Moon in Scorpio/Venus in Pisces

Intimacy plays a large part in the lives of these highly sexed, romantic individuals. Your emotional nature is so complex that your love affairs can be as turbulent as they are passionate; you may display a poignant vulnerability one moment, and become possessive and demanding the next. Despite your strong libido, sexual satisfaction is not the primary focus of your lovemaking. You crave a spiritual union that connects you to your partner—body and soul.

Combinations of the Moon in Sagittarius

Moon in Sagittarius/Venus in Aries

A whirlwind of passion surrounds you as your impetuous nature propels you into acts of romantic daring. For you, good sex includes innovation and as much excitement as you can generate. In bed and out, you're more aware of your own feelings than those of your significant other and you may not even realize when your partner is unable to keep up with you. Your intense vitality and love of adventure sets such a hectic pace that your mate can often do little more than hang on for dear life. Although you give yourself wholeheartedly to love, your restlessness and impatience may cause you to leave if you feel stifled.

Moon in Sagittarius/Venus in Taurus

You long to settle down and bask in the emotional security of a close relationship, but as soon as this happens, you may find yourself feeling restless. Making love is the most natural thing in the world to you, and your fiery libido demands lots of sexual activity. Your ideal mate not only understands the urgency of your erotic desires, but shares them.

Moon in Sagittarius/Venus in Gemini

In relationships, you're passionate, generous, full of fun, and eager for love. Friendship and companionship mean as much to you as love and sex, however excessive displays of emotion tend to scare you off. You love trying new things and—to your way of thinking—a permanent romantic alliance can put severe limitations on your ability to experience the richness and variety of life. Since outdoor romantic encounters appeal to you, spontaneous lovemaking in open spaces gets your erotic juices flowing.

Moon in Sagittarius/Venus in Cancer

You're a loving person who often has a hard time in close relationships. Part of you just wants to stay in and cuddle by the fireside, while another part of you longs to go out and socialize. Your ideal mate knows how to maintain a sense of freedom within an atmosphere of togetherness. You're warm and sexy in bed, and the intimacy you share with your partner becomes a cozy sanctuary away from the world.

Moon in Sagittarius/Venus in Leo

Dashing and dramatic by nature, you throw yourself into romance with such enthusiasm that you seem to be playing a role in a show. For you, love is everything when it's happening, yet you start feeling nervous if the relationship gets too confining. Sociable and witty, you enjoy amusement in its various forms, and your friendly openness attracts all manner of fun-loving companions. Behind closed doors, your physical prowess and fiery libido provide sexual endurance into the wee hours.

Moon in Sagittarius/Venus in Virgo

People with this combination typically resist the temptation to plunge into a serious relationship until they're absolutely sure the person in question is right for them. However, your sex drive is strong and once you decide to commit you're an energetic, passionate lover. You are kindhearted and caring, but also idealistic. Your craving for perfection can create a huge gap between your dreams of love and everyday life. For you, a courtship that begins with friendship and intellectual rapport has the best chance of blossoming into true love.

Moon in Sagittarius/Venus in Libra

Fun-loving and sociable, you aren't overly inclined to stay at home and snuggle up in front of the TV with your lover. You want to be out on the town, where you can do exciting things and meet interesting new people. Nevertheless, when you do stay at home, you're a skilled and considerate lover, eager to make your bed partner happy. The romantic Libra in you yearns for a committed union, but your independent Sagittarian Moon detests being tied down. For the best of both worlds, you need a mate who not only loves you, but also shares your wanderlust.

Moon in Sagittarius/Venus in Scorpio

Your devilish charm draws many suitors, and it may seem that romance for you is nothing more than a series of adventures. However, nothing could be further from the truth. Actually, you're a passionate idealist and take love very seriously. Once you're involved, you quickly dispense with your *laissez-faire* attitude and behave in a possessive and controlling manner. Your appetite for sensual pleasures is strong, and you enjoy making love outdoors under the stars.

Moon in Sagittarius/Venus in Sagittarius

You regard love as a grand and glorious experience, yet your need for freedom and independence makes loyalty difficult to sustain. Since you live to party and flirt, you may find a series of romantic escapades a lot more to your liking than a serious, long-term union. The suitor who introduces you to new experiences has an edge with you. Sex for you is an extension of your joyous life force, and your bedroom romps are filled with playful energy and warm affection. However, coping with everyday realities is not your forte, and any relationship that makes too many demands won't last long.

Moon in Sagittarius/Venus in Capricorn

In matters of the heart, you're a unique combination of idealism and pragmatism. While a steady, enduring relationship suits you on many levels, you also crave a certain amount of excitement. Fun-loving without being frivolous, you're gregarious up to a point. Your serious side is more concerned with practical achievements than socializing. Driven by the same desire to succeed in the bedroom as in other areas of your life, you work hard to please your lover.

Moon in Sagittarius/Venus in Aquarius

An open-minded free spirit, you're always on the lookout for new adventures and enjoy being with people who expand your range of experience. The seeker in you likes experimenting with love, and you generally hold an "anything goes" attitude toward romance and sexuality. You've had your share of unconventional liaisons, and wouldn't want it any other way. Although your feelings of love and affection tend to remain constant, you require a lot of freedom in an intimate relationship and settling down with one person may not be right for you.

Moon in Sagittarius/Venus in Pisces

People born under this combination of the Moon and Venus are warmhearted, generous, and caring. Full of life and excitement, you enjoy being on the move, meeting lots of new people, and having many opportunities for fun. Your dreamy approach to love and romance is part of your charm, and easily captivates potential lovers. Your ideal mate responds to your unique, highly intuitive style of loving with grateful enthusiasm.

Combinations of the Moon in Capricorn

Moon in Capricorn/Venus in Aries

People born under this combination tend to be emotionally cool and restrained and not particularly accessible—even to those closest to them. In the bedroom, you're upfront about your physical needs and desires. Although strongly sexed and ardent, you are quite capable of controlling and directing your passion when it suits you. Because you're something of a workaholic, love, marriage, and even sex sometimes take a backseat to your career plans.

Moon in Capricorn/Venus in Taurus

Because of your ability to stay calm when everyone around you is upset, you sometimes come across as cool and calculating. Actually, you're quite emotional, but aren't always willing to let your feelings show. At heart you're a secret romantic, with a desperate desire to be loved and understood. Naturally sensual and passionate, you are uniquely responsive to erotic stimuli. However, in addition to physical lovemaking you also need affection and emotional reassurance from a caring mate. Once you feel truly secure, you are the most considerate and devoted of partners.

Moon in Capricorn/Venus in Gemini

Your wit, charm, and brilliant sense of humor make you the life of any party. However, deep down you're anything but frivolous. In addition to being ardent and affectionate, your ideal mate is smart and entertaining. He or she should get as much pleasure from debating and sharing ideas as from lovemaking. In the bedroom, lighthearted fun and sexy banter bring out your hidden sensuality.

Moon in Capricorn/Venus in Cancer

Those with this combination don't like to appear vulnerable; you need to know that you're the only one in control of your destiny. Trust doesn't come easy to you, and you tend to retreat when you feel insecure. However, once your love and confidence have been won, you are likely to remain loyal and devoted forever. Between the sheets, you're passionate, yet tender and controlled. Sexual expertise is important to you and, like everything else in your life, you'll spare no effort to achieve it.

Moon in Capricorn/Venus in Leo

You enjoy being a star, and the lion inside you turns wildly flirtatious when your passions are ignited. Although you present a dazzling image of confidence to the world, it is mainly bravado. Deep down you're rather insecure, and a bit of ego boosting from your partner is always welcome. Your ideal lover does whatever is necessary to please you—both in and out of the bedroom. In return, you'll spare no effort satisfying his or her desires.

Moon in Capricorn/Venus in Virgo

You may appear cool and controlled on the outside, but within yourself you're kindhearted and emotionally vulnerable. As a lover, few other members of the zodiacal family are as loyal, caring, and dependable as you. However, physical chemistry alone isn't enough to lure you into a romantic relationship. You want a life partner whose ambitions and worldview complement your own.

Moon in Capricorn/Venus in Libra

A close relationship is important to your well-being and, when you find the right person you're capable of total loyalty and devotion. An idealist, you appreciate the charm and glamour of an old-fashioned courtship. Domestic strife turns you off and, once involved, you want a harmonious home life. The elegant suitor who is provocative rather than overt in his or her attempts at seduction has the edge with you. An attentive lover who sets the mood with affectionate gestures in a romantic ambiance stirs your refined sensibilities.

Moon in Capricorn/Venus in Scorpio

In a romantic union, you're a sensual and passionate lover, and need a partner whose libido and desire for intimacy matches your own. Since love is an all-or-nothing proposition for you, the words *casual* and *sex* don't belong together as far as you're concerned. A relationship with you isn't likely to be either light or easy, because you can be moody, controlling, and possessive. However, once you find a mate you can count on, you'll do everything you possibly can to make love last a lifetime.

Moon in Capricorn/Venus in Sagittarius

A paradox when it comes to love, you can be playful and flirty one moment, absolutely serious the next. In youth, you may engage in some lusty experimental affairs, but will eventually want to settle down to a stable romantic union. In bed, you enjoy trying new ways to enhance sensual pleasure. High-energy lovemaking takes you and your mate to orgiastic peaks that strengthen your bond and increase your feelings of intimacy.

Moon in Capricorn/Venus in Capricorn

Your deepest need is to be loved, but you're cautious regarding your emotions, preferring to hold back rather than appear vulnerable. However, when you trust someone enough to let down your guard, you make a sensual, dependable life partner. Too much of a realist to expect perfection, you want a mate who lives up to your high standards. You value the individual who is responsible and hardworking, and offer the same qualities in return. You may not be the most romantic lover, but what you lack in glamour you make up for in passion and endurance.

Moon in Capricorn/Venus in Aquarius

In an intimate union, a superficial air of detachment masks your deep devotion to your partner. You crave affection and understanding, yet prefer to avoid overt displays of emotion. Even though intimacy is not your strong point, your loyalty and dependability outweigh any emotional shortcomings you may possess. In the bedroom, you willingly follow your strong need for physical fulfillment wherever it leads you. Even so, you're extremely particular about who you get involved with. You are especially likely to rebuff a pushy lover who attempts to control you.

Moon in Capricorn/Venus in Pisces

You are idealistic, but also responsible and devoted. Generous and protective of your loved ones, your sensitive feelings can be hurt if you sense that your help isn't appreciated. Despite the cool self-sufficiency of Capricorn, the part of your love nature that is influenced by Pisces craves affection and is never truly happy without it. An old-fashioned romantic courtship stirs your libido and plays into your fantasies. Your ideal lover is the one who can charm both the starry-eyed romantic and the realist in you.

Combinations of the Moon in Aquarius

Moon in Aquarius/Venus in Aries

Despite your independent spirit, you're very much a people-person; your magnetic personality draws others to you. In love, you can be as ardent and romantic as any other Aries, but the emotional detachment of Aquarius keeps you from becoming overly intimate. You enjoy variety in the bedroom, and a free-spirited, uninhibited lover ignites your libido. Your sexual imagination is powerful, if not fully accessible, but your ideal bedmate knows how to turn your fantasies into realities.

Moon in Aquarius/Venus in Taurus

You want the security of a close relationship, but have an independent spirit that resists intimacy. However, you understand your own quirks where matters of the heart are concerned, and your marvelous sense of humor prompts you to joke about your foibles. You bring fun and spontaneity into the bedroom, and your hearty appetite for tactile pleasure makes you a master of sensual foreplay.

Moon in Aquarius/Venus in Gemini

This combination brings together the two signs that are most wary of emotional vulnerability. You're loyal to those you love, but won't tolerate restrictions on your freedom. While you may think you want the closeness and passionate intensity of an intimate union, you're actually attracted by intellectual companionship and mutual understanding. Even in the bedroom, sex is not always the first thing on your mind. Nevertheless, when you do get around to lovemaking, you're an innovative lover and variety in sexual expression turns you on.

Moon in Aquarius/Venus in Cancer

Subtle in your approach, you're not likely to broadcast your intentions until you feel certain that you're on firm ground. Cancer prefers dropping little hints in order to gauge the other person's level of interest, before making a move. Whereas Cancer makes you cuddly and loving, the influence of Aquarius can make you appear aloof and distant. Cancer longs for commitment and permanence, but unconventional Aquarius tends to prefer independence. In love, you are passionate and romantic, and willing to do whatever it takes to pleasure your lover.

Moon in Aquarius/Venus in Leo

For you, romance needs to be full of fun and glamour. Outgoing and genuinely interested in people, you enjoy parties and gatherings where you get a chance to turn on the charm. Loyal and sincere in your relationships, close friendship is so important to you that you sometimes confuse it with love. An intelligent, attentive partner with an original approach keeps you intrigued. You enjoy lavish theatrics in the bedroom, and splurging on silky bedclothes and sexy attire helps you set the scene for a delightful night of lovemaking.

Moon in Aquarius/Venus in Virgo

You are uncomfortable with effusive people who act out their feelings in an emotional manner, and you shy away from public displays of affection. However, behind closed doors Aquarius's love of erotic novelty quickly overcomes Virgo's hesitancy. In the bedroom, you thoroughly enjoy sexual experimentation, readily adding whatever makes you feel good to your between-the-sheets repertoire. Companionship and friendship are important to you, and keeping an intimate relationship on an even keel matters more to you than wild, passionate lovemaking. Your ideal mate is as intelligent, rational, and undemonstrative in public as you.

Moon in Aquarius/Venus in Libra

In this Moon/Venus combination, Libra's tendency to think in pairs is somewhat diminished by Aquarian independence. Although affectionate and caring, you project an airy detachment even in your most intimate alliances. You hate the thought of being restricted and in love, and you can be impulsive when attraction hits you. A born flirt, you zero in on the object of your interest and make your desires known in a subtle but undeniable manner. In the bedroom, you're an extremely smooth, adventurous, and satisfying lover. Your ideal relationship merges romance and sexuality with friendship and intellectual rapport.

Moon in Aquarius/Venus in Scorpio

In close relationships you blow hot and cold and your moods swings can be extreme. Scorpio's emotional intensity does not mesh well with the intellectuality of lunar Aquarius. Although you crave sexual fulfillment, you also need a lover you can talk to. Moreover, you may feel torn between the water bearer's love of freedom and the scorpion's desire for a deeply committed partnership. Although your ardor is unpredictable, once you get going few are capable of matching the passion of your lustier moments.

Moon in Aquarius/Venus in Sagittarius

Basically optimistic and adventurous, you approach relationships with an open mind and heart. Physically sensual and passionate, you're emotionally cooler than other Venusian archers. In a close union, companionship and mental rapport are important to you and, since your intimate unions tend to be more idealistic than practical, you may spend more time chasing your dream than actually settling down to a real-life partnership. Future-oriented, when a romance is over, you move on without regrets, and never look back.

Moon in Aquarius/Venus in Capricorn

Although you value your independence, you really don't like being alone. Once involved in an intimate union, you crave love and affection yet you hold back until you feel totally secure. Even then, you rarely surrender to chaotic emotions. Behind closed doors, however, your physical passion and sensuality emerge full-blown. The rough and tumble of ardent lovemaking invigorates you and makes you feel as though you've had a lovely vacation away from the practical considerations of everyday life.

Moon in Aquarius/Venus in Aquarius

When it comes to love, you march to a totally different drummer. Society's conventions and other people's opinions matter very little to you; you make your own rules. Since you require lots of freedom and independence, you're not likely to put up with possessiveness, jealousy, or anyone who is overly dependent on you. As open-minded about sex as about everything else, you enjoy experimenting between the sheets.

Moon in Aquarius/Venus in Pisces

People with this combination often have their heads in the clouds, and are prone to base close relationships on romantic ideals rather than practical realities. In an intimate union, you're generous, caring, and considerate. However, airy Aquarius makes you more independent than other fish.

As a result, there is a part of you that you keep only to yourself. Romantic fantasy probably plays a large part in your love life and, since you're totally uninhibited in bed, anything new or different intrigues you.

Combinations of the Moon in Pisces

Moon in Pisces/Venus in Aries

Problems may arise because of your tendency to place your lover on a pedestal; eventually your beloved fails to live up to your idealistic notions and falls from grace. Passionate, romantic, dreamy, and sensitive, you require a considerable amount of pampering from your lover. In return, you're cognizant of your partner's desires—sexual and otherwise—and are more than happy to fulfill them. There is a playful, adventurous, even bawdy side to your love nature that is only fully expressed in the privacy of the bedroom.

Moon in Pisces/Venus in Taurus

In intimate relationships you're the consummate romantic, but you enjoy your creature comforts and realize you can't live on love alone. Even if you fall head-over-heels, you somehow manage to keep your feet on the ground. Loyal, caring, sensual, and affectionate, as a lover you're both giving and responsive. However, you can also be jealous and possessive.

Moon in Pisces/Venus in Gemini

Although those born under this combination want the grounding that partnership offers, they fear emotional vulnerability. When you do get seriously involved, however, you make a delightfully romantic lover. Nevertheless, your mind is your most sensitive erogenous zone. Your fluency with playful, sexy banter makes you a seductive flirt. You channel lots of energy into communication, and whispering sweet nothings and naughty ideas in your partner's ear during lovemaking turns you on.

Moon in Pisces/Venus in Cancer

In close relationships, you are cautious and vulnerable, yet also enormously caring and generous. You flourish with a strong partner who makes you feel safe and secure and encourages you in all your efforts. You enjoy your creature comforts and, since you're not very daring, you prefer sex in your own bed. However, once there you use your creative imagination to invent enchanting erotic fantasies and role-playing games that can be as stimulating and exciting as actual adventures.

Moon in Pisces/Venus in Leo

Naturally charismatic and empathetic, you pour your heart and soul into an intimate union. A romantic and a dreamer, you have a strong picture in your mind of what love looks like. However, you're prone to falling for the type of lover who turns out to not be what you'd imagined. Yet, after a short period of feeling sorry for yourself, you bounce back more optimistic than ever and willingly try again. In the bedroom, you're capable of great passion, and your lovemaking style is steamy and dramatic. Although loyal and devoted, you can't feign what you don't really feel. When the spark goes out of a relationship, you would rather end it than spend years being miserable.

Moon in Pisces/Venus in Virgo

In a close relationship, you want complete acceptance from your beloved, which is exactly what you're prepared to give in return. Although picky and rather demanding, you're too sensitive to inflict undo criticism on your partner. While a part of you prefers a relationship built on common interests and intellectual rapport, you also want romance and a touch of magic. If you don't get it you may retreat into the fantasy world of your imagination. Yet, where sex is concerned, you refuse to romanticize your physical desires, and your clear awareness of your own lusty nature makes you a formidable lover.

Moon in Pisces/Venus in Libra

Since you adore being half of a couple, loving relationships are the seminal experiences in your life. Once involved, you identify with your mate and his or her best interests. Because you seek harmony in all your alliances, you routinely solicit the other person's views and opinion and then reformulate your own to conform, thus avoiding conflict. In a romantic union, your tendency is to abandon yourself completely to love. As a result, you are extremely versatile and compliant in the bedroom. Whatever pleases your partner makes you happy as well.

Moon in Pisces/Venus in Scorpio

People with this combination are highly sensitive, with a psychic-like understanding of the unspoken subtleties in relationships. Your sultry bedroom eyes lure potential suitors, and your warm, pleasant manner reels them in. When your feelings are involved—which they are in virtually everything you do—you don't do things halfway. As a lover you're extremely loyal, generous, and caring, but also needy, jealous, and possessive.

Moon in Pisces/Venus in Sagittarius

Kind-hearted and unselfish, those born under this combination tend to see the best in everyone. You're genuinely interested in broadening your knowledge of your environment and the people in it, but half the time you live in a dream world. As a result, you may fall hopelessly in love, idealize your significant other, and then give into despair because he or she is unable to live up to your mythological ideal. You approach romance—and sex—with an innocent exuberance that makes your lover's heart race.

Moon in Pisces/Venus in Capricorn

You have a romantic side, but try not to let it get the better of you. You long for a meaningful relationship, but your sensitive feelings are easily hurt and you may be afraid to take a chance on love. Even so, once involved you're caring and devoted, and tend to anticipate your partner's needs before he or she is even aware of them. Although somewhat reclusive, you enjoy the company of a partner who is more outgoing and sociable. In private, your cuddly warmth and sexual stamina create many moments of treasured intimacy.

Moon in Pisces/Venus in Aquarius

Love highlights the paradox between your innate romanticism and rational realism. Even in your most intimate relationships, you maintain an air of Aquarian aloofness that is often at odds with the emotionality of your Pisces Moon. Your mixture of spontaneous warmth and empathy with cool-headed detachment makes you a wonderful friend, but can sometimes be rather puzzling to a lover. Nevertheless, you make up for your enigmatic behavior in the bedroom, where you offer warmth and understanding along with intense passion and a complete willingness to go along with whatever your partner wants.

Moon in Pisces/Venus in Pisces

You are the quintessential romantic. For you, love is the stuff of poetry, dreams, and fairy tales. Your deep feelings are easily engaged—and easily wounded—and your gentle, tenderhearted love nature requires tons of affection, attention, encouragement, and emotional support. You give all of yourself to love, and will readily sacrifice your own desires for those of your mate. Yet, with your wonderful imagination, you make even the most ordinary sexual union seem glamorous and exciting.

Appendix A
Determining Your Sun Sign

AS YOUR SUN SIGN IS DETERMINED by the position of the sun on the day you were born, the only way to figure out your sun sign is to find the sign the corresponds with your birthday in the chart below.

SUN SIGN CHART

Date of Birth	Sun Sign	Quality	Element
March 21–April 19	Aries (Ram)	Cardinal	Fire
April 20–May 20	Taurus (Bull)	Fixed	Earth
May 21–June 20	Gemini (Twins)	Mutable	Air
June 21–July 22	Cancer (Crab)	Cardinal	Water
July 23–August 22	Leo (Lion)	Fixed	Fire
August 23–September 22	Virgo (Virgin)	Mutable	Earth
September 23–October 22	Libra (Scales)	Cardinal	Air
October 23–November 21	Scorpio (Scorpion)	Fixed	Water
November 22–December 21	Sagittarius (Archer)	Mutable	Fire
December 22–January 20	Capricorn (Goat)	Cardinal	Earth
January 21–February 18	Aquarius (Water-Carrier)	Fixed	Air
February 19–March 20	Pisces (Fish)	Mutable	Water

Born on a Cusp?

The dates given in the Sun Sign Chart are only an approximation, because the Sun does not enter each of the signs on the same day or time every year. If you were born on a cusp (a day when the Sun changes signs) you'll need to determine which sign the Sun was in at the time you were born. As long as you know your time of birth, you can have an accurate horoscope chart drawn up by an astrologer. You can also obtain a free copy of your birth chart online. Check out AstroDienst (*www.astro.com*), Café Astrology (*www.cafeastrology.com*), or Astrolabe (*www.alabe.com*) for more information.

If you were born on a cusp day, but don't know your exact birth time, you may never know for sure which Sun sign is the correct one. In this case you should read the interpretation for the adjacent sign as well as the one for your birthday, to see which one is a better fit.

Appendix B
Determining Your Moon Sign

THE MOON TAKES APPROXIMATELY TWO AND A HALF DAYS to pass through each sign, and it completes one zodiac circuit in roughly twenty-seven days. It returns to the same zodiacal position on the same date every nineteen years. This predictable lunar cycle makes it possible for astrologers to create tables that you can use to locate your Moon sign.

How to Use the Moon Sign Tables

Beginning with Table One, locate the line that contains your birth year. Then go to your birth month at the top of the chart, and run your finger down that column until you reach the astrological sign that is on the same line as your birth year. This is the sign occupied by the Moon on the first day of the month of your birth.

Next go to Table Two and find the number of the day you were born. The number next to this day in the Add column is the number of signs that you need to count through to reach your Moon sign.

Finally, go to Table Three. Starting with the sign you found for your birth year and month in Table One, count off the number of signs you found in the Add column next to your birthday in Table Two. When using Table Three, be sure to count through the signs in a continuous loop, so number one follows on from number twelve.

Example: To find the Moon sign for someone born on April 26, 1989:

From Table One: On April 1, 1989 the Moon was in Aquarius

From Table Two: Day 26, add eleven signs.

From Table Three: Count off eleven signs after Aquarius (number eleven). Therefore you begin with Pisces (#12) and count through to Capricorn (#10).

Result: On April 26, 1989 the Moon was in Capricorn.

Although this method for locating the Moon's sign is fairly accurate, if you find that you disagree with the characteristics of the resulting sign it may be that you were born on a cusp day, when the Moon changed signs. If this is the case, read the interpretation for the adjacent sign to see if it is a better fit.

MOON TABLE ONE: SIGN CHART 1930–2015

Year of Birth						Jan	Feb	Mar	Apr	May	Jun	Jul	Aug	Sep	Oct	Nov	Dec
	1939	1958	1977	1996	2015	Tau	Can	Can	Vir	Lib	Sag	Cap	Aqu	Ari	Tau	Can	Leo
	1940	1959	1978	1997		Lib	Sco	Sag	Cap	Aqu	Ari	Tau	Can	Leo	Vir	Sco	Sag
	1941	1960	1979	1998		Aqu	Ari	Ari	Gem	Can	Leo	Vir	Sco	Cap	Aqu	Ari	Tau
	1942	1961	1980	1999		Gem	Leo	Leo	Lib	Sco	Cap	Aqu	Ari	Tau	Gem	Leo	Vir
	1943	1962	1981	2000		Sco	Sag	Cap	Aqu	Ari	Tau	Gem	Leo	Lib	Sco	Sag	Cap
	1944	1963	1982	2001		Pis	Tau	Tau	Can	Leo	Lib	Sco	Sag	Aqu	Pis	Tau	Gem
	1945	1964	1983	2002		Leo	Vir	Lib	Sco	Sag	Aqu	Pis	Tau	Can	Leo	Vir	Lib
	1946	1965	1984	2003		Sag	Cap	Aqu	Pis	Tau	Gem	Leo	Vir	Sco	Sag	Aqu	Pis
	1947	1966	1985	2004		Ari	Gem	Gem	Leo	Vir	Sco	Sag	Aqu	Pis	Ari	Gem	Can
	1948	1967	1986	2005		Vir	Sco	Sco	Cap	Aqu	Pis	Tau	Gem	Leo	Vir	Lib	Sag
1930	1949	1968	1987	2006		Cap	Pis	Pis	Tau	Gem	Leo	Bir	Sco	Sag	Cap	Pis	Ari
1931	1950	1969	1988	2007		Tau	Can	Can	Vir	Lib	Sag	Cap	Pis	Ari	Gem	Can	Leo
1932	1951	1970	1989	2008		Lib	Sag	Sag	Aqu	Pis	Tau	Gem	Can	Vir	Lib	Sag	Cap
1933	1952	1971	1990	2009		Pis	Ari	Tau	Gem	Can	Vir	Lib	Sag	Cap	Aqu	Ari	Tau
1934	1953	1972	1991	2010		Can	Vir	Vir	Lib	Sag	Cap	Pis	Ari	Gem	Can	Vir	Lib
1935	1954	1973	1992	2011		Sco	Cap	Cap	Pis	Ari	Gem	Can	Vir	Sco	Sag	Cap	Aqu
1936	1955	1974	1993	2012		Ari	Tau	Gem	Leo	Vir	Lib	Sco	Cap	Pis	Ari	Tau	Can
1937	1956	1975	1994	2013		Leo	Lib	Lib	Sag	Cap	Pis	Ari	Tau	Can	Leo	Lib	Sco
1938	1957	1976	1995	2014		Cap	Aqu	Pis	Ari	Tau	Can	Leo	Lib	Sco	Cap	Aqu	Ari

MOON TABLE TWO:
NUMBER OF SIGNS TO ADD FOR EACH DAY OF THE MONTH

Day	Add
1	0
2	1
3	1
4	1
5	2
6	2
7	3
8	3
9	4
10	4
11	5
12	5
13	5
14	6
15	6
16	7
17	7
18	8
19	8
20	9
21	9
22	10
23	10
24	10
25	11
26	11
27	12
28	12
29	1
30	1
31	2

MOON TABLE THREE: SIGNS OF THE ZODIAC

Number	Corresponding Sign
1	Aries
2	Taurus
3	Gemini
4	Cancer
5	Leo
6	Virgo
7	Libra
8	Scorpio
9	Sagittarius
10	Capricorn
11	Aquarius
12	Pisces

Appendix C

Mars and Venus Ephemeris Tables

USE THE MARS AND VENUS EPHEMERIS TABLES in this Appendix to determine the sign positions of Mars and Venus on the day you were born. These tables list the dates and times that each of the planets changed signs during the years 1930–2015. To determine the placements of Mars and Venus on the day you were born, locate your birth date or the date just prior to your birthday in the appropriate table.

Example of finding Mars's placement on April 26, 1987:

04-05-1987	11:38 AM	Gem
05-20-1987	10:01 PM	Cap

Since the indicated birthday falls after 04-05-1987, but before 05-20-1987, the individual's Mars is in Gemini (Gem).

All of the ephemeris listings are for 12 Noon in New York City (Eastern Time Zone). If you were born in a different time zone, simply adjust for the number of hours east or west of New York. In the example given above, if the person was born in Los Angeles (Pacific Time Zone), Mars would have changed signs three hours earlier than in New York, changing the calculation to the signs below:

04-05-1987	08:38 AM	Gem
05-20-1987	07:01 PM	Can

Alternative Method

If you'd rather not be bothered with calculations, skip this section altogether, and have your natal chart done online. With a horoscope chart erected for your time and place of birth, you'll know the correct placements of the Moon and Venus, even if you were born on a cusp day in a different time zone. Check out: AstroDienst (*www.astro.com*), Café Astrology (*www.cafeastrology.com*), and Astrolabe (*www.alabe.com*) to create your chart online.

MARS SIGN POSITIONS 1930–2015

Date of Birth	Time of Birth	Mars Sign
02-06-1930	01:21 PM	Aqu
03-17-1930	12:55 am	Pis
04-24-1930	12:27 pm	Ari
06-02-1930	10:16 pm	Tau
07-14-1930	07:54 am	Gem
08-28-1930	06:27 am	Can
10-20-1930	09:45 am	Leo
06-10-1931	09:58 am	Vir
08-01-1931	11:38 am	Lib
09-17-1931	03:43 am	Sco
10-30-1931	07:46 am	Sag
12-09-1931	10:11 pm	Cap
01-17-1932	07:35 pm	Aqu
02-24-1932	09:36 pm	Pis
04-03-1932	02:02 am	Ari

Date of Birth	Time of Birth	Mars Sign
05-12-1932	05:54 am	Tau
06-22-1932	04:19 am	Gem
08-04-1932	02:52 pm	Can
09-20-1932	02:43 pm	Leo
11-13-1932	04:25 pm	Vir
07-06-1933	05:04 pm	Lib
08-26-1933	01:34 am	Sco
10-09-1933	06:35 am	Sag
11-19-1933	02:18 am	Cap
12-27-1933	10:43 pm	Aqu
02-03-1934	11:13 pm	Pis
03-14-1934	04:09 am	Ari
04-22-1934	10:41 am	Tau
06-02-1934	11:21 am	Gem
07-15-1934	04:33 pm	Can
08-30-1934	08:43 am	Leo
10-17-1934	11:59 pm	Vir
12-11-1934	04:32 am	Lib
07-29-1935	12:32 pm	Sco
09-16-1935	07:59 am	Sag
10-28-1935	01:22 pm	Cap
12-06-1935	11:34 pm	Aqu
01-14-1936	08:59 am	Pis
02-21-1936	11:09 pm	Ari
04-01-1936	04:30 pm	Tau
05-13-1936	04:17 am	Gem
06-25-1936	04:53 pm	Can

Date of Birth	Time of Birth	Mars Sign
08-10-1936	04:42 am	Leo
09-26-1936	09:52 am	Vir
11-14-1936	09:53 am	Lib
01-05-1937	03:39 pm	Sco
03-12-1937	10:17 pm	Sag
09-30-1937	04:08 am	Cap
11-11-1937	01:31 pm	Aqu
12-21-1937	12:46 pm	Pis
01-30-1938	07:44 am	Ari
03-12-1938	02:48 am	Tau
04-23-1938	01:39 pm	Gem
06-06-1938	08:28 pm	Can
07-22-1938	05:26 pm	Leo
09-07-1938	03:23 pm	Vir
10-25-1938	01:20 am	Lib
12-11-1938	06:25 pm	Sco
01-29-1939	04:49 am	Sag
03-21-1939	02:26 pm	Cap
05-24-1939	07:17 pm	Aqu
11-19-1939	10:57 am	Pis
01-03-1940	07:05 pm	Ari
02-16-1940	08:54 pm	Tau
04-01-1940	01:41 pm	Gem
05-17-1940	09:46 am	Can
07-03-1940	05:32 am	Leo
08-19-1940	10:58 am	Vir
10-05-1940	09:21 am	Lib

Date of Birth	Time of Birth	Mars Sign
11-20-1940	12:16 pm	Sco
01-04-1941	02:43 pm	Sag
02-17-1941	06:32 pm	Cap
04-02-1941	06:46 am	Aqu
05-16-1941	12:04 am	Pis
07-02-1941	12:16 am	Ari
01-11-1942	05:20 pm	Tau
03-07-1942	03:04 am	Gem
04-26-1942	01:18 am	Can
06-13-1942	10:56 pm	Leo
08-01-1942	03:27 am	Vir
09-17-1942	05:11 am	Lib
11-01-1942	05:36 pm	Sco
12-15-1942	11:51 am	Sag
01-26-1943	02:10 pm	Cap
03-08-1943	07:42 am	Aqu
04-17-1943	05:26 am	Pis
05-27-1943	04:25 am	Ari
07-07-1943	06:05 pm	Tau
08-23-1943	06:58 pm	Gem
03-28-1944	04:54 am	Can
05-22-1944	09:16 am	Leo
07-11-1944	09:55 pm	Vir
08-28-1944	07:23 pm	Lib
10-13-1944	07:10 am	Sco
11-25-1944	11:12 am	Sag
01-05-1945	02:31 pm	Cap

Date of Birth	Time of Birth	Mars Sign
02-14-1945	04:58 am	Aqu
03-24-1945	10:44 pm	Pis
05-02-1945	03:29 pm	Ari
06-11-1945	06:53 am	Tau
07-23-1945	03:59 am	Gem
09-07-1945	03:56 pm	Can
11-11-1945	04:06 pm	Leo
06-20-1946	03:32 am	Vir
08-09-1946	08:17 am	Lib
09-24-1946	11:35 am	Sco
11-06-1946	01:23 pm	Sag
12-17-1946	05:56 am	Cap
01-25-1947	06:45 am	Aqu
03-04-1947	11:47 am	Pis
04-11-1947	06:03 pm	Ari
05-20-1947	10:40 pm	Tau
06-30-1947	10:34 pm	Gem
08-13-1947	04:26 pm	Can
09-30-1947	09:30 pm	Leo
12-01-1947	06:42 am	Vir
07-17-1948	12:26 am	Lib
09-03-1948	08:58 am	Sco
10-17-1948	12:44 am	Sag
11-26-1948	04:59 pm	Cap
01-04-1949	12:50 pm	Aqu
02-11-1949	01:06 pm	Pis
03-21-1949	05:02 pm	Ari

Date of Birth	Time of Birth	Mars Sign
04-29-1949	09:33 pm	Tau
06-09-1949	07:57 pm	Gem
07-23-1949	12:54 am	Can
09-06-1949	11:51 pm	Leo
10-26-1949	07:59 pm	Vir
12-26-1949	12:23 am	Lib
08-10-1950	11:48 am	Sco
09-25-1950	02:49 pm	Sag
11-06-1950	01:40 am	Cap
12-15-1950	03:59 am	Aqu
01-22-1951	08:06 am	Pis
03-01-1951	05:03 pm	Ari
04-10-1951	04:37 am	Tau
05-21-1951	10:32 am	Gem
07-03-1951	06:42 pm	Can
08-18-1951	05:55 am	Leo
10-04-1951	07:20 pm	Vir
11-24-1951	01:11 am	Lib
01-19-1952	08:32 pm	Sco
08-27-1952	01:53 pm	Sag
10-11-1952	11:45 pm	Cap
11-21-1952	02:40 pm	Aqu
12-30-1952	04:36 pm	Pis
02-07-1953	08:07 pm	Ari
03-20-1953	01:54 am	Tau
05-01-1953	01:08 am	Gem
06-13-1953	10:49 pm	Can

Date of Birth	Time of Birth	Mars Sign
07-29-1953	02:25 pm	Leo
09-14-1953	12:59 pm	Vir
11-01-1953	09:19 am	Lib
12-20-1953	06:22 am	Sco
02-09-1954	02:18 pm	Sag
04-12-1954	11:28 am	Cap
10-21-1954	07:02 am	Aqu
12-04-1954	02:42 am	Pis
01-14-1955	11:34 pm	Ari
02-26-1955	05:22 am	Tau
04-10-1955	06:09 pm	Gem
05-25-1955	07:50 pm	Can
07-11-1955	04:22 am	Leo
08-27-1955	05:14 am	Vir
10-13-1955	06:20 am	Lib
11-28-1955	08:33 pm	Sco
01-13-1956	09:28 pm	Sag
02-28-1956	03:05 pm	Cap
04-14-1956	06:41 pm	Aqu
06-03-1956	02:52 am	Pis
12-06-1956	06:24 am	Ari
01-28-1957	09:19 am	Tau
03-17-1957	04:34 pm	Gem
05-04-1957	10:22 am	Can
06-21-1957	07:18 am	Leo
08-08-1957	12:28 am	Vir
09-23-1957	11:31 pm	Lib

Date of Birth	Time of Birth	Mars Sign
11-08-1957	04:04 pm	Sco
12-22-1957	08:30 pm	Sag
02-03-1958	01:57 pm	Cap
03-17-1958	02:11 am	Aqu
04-26-1958	09:31 pm	Pis
06-07-1958	01:21 am	Ari
07-21-1958	02:03 am	Tau
09-21-1958	12:22 am	Gem
04-10-1959	04:46 am	Can
05-31-1959	09:25 pm	Leo
07-20-1959	06:04 am	Vir
09-05-1959	05:47 pm	Lib
10-21-1959	04:40 am	Sco
12-03-1959	01:09 pm	Sag
01-13-1960	12:00 pm	Cap
02-22-1960	11:12 pm	Aqu
04-02-1960	01:24 am	Pis
05-11-1960	02:19 am	Ari
06-20-1960	04:05 am	Tau
08-01-1960	11:32 pm	Gem
09-20-1960	11:07 pm	Can
05-05-1961	08:13 pm	Leo
06-28-1961	06:48 pm	Vir
08-16-1961	07:42 pm	Lib
10-01-1961	03:02 pm	Sco
11-13-1961	04:51 pm	Sag
12-24-1961	12:50 pm	Cap

Date of Birth	Time of Birth	Mars Sign
02-01-1962	06:07 pm	Aqu
03-12-1962	02:59 am	Pis
04-19-1962	11:59 am	Ari
05-28-1962	06:47 pm	Tau
07-08-1962	10:50 pm	Gem
08-22-1962	06:37 am	Can
10-11-1962	06:54 pm	Leo
06-03-1963	01:30 am	Vir
07-26-1963	11:15 pm	Lib
09-12-1963	04:11 am	Sco
10-25-1963	12:32 pm	Sag
12-05-1963	04:03 am	Cap
01-13-1964	01:14 am	Aqu
02-20-1964	02:33 am	Pis
03-29-1964	06:25 am	Ari
05-07-1964	09:41 am	Tau
06-17-1964	06:43 am	Gem
07-30-1964	01:22 pm	Can
09-15-1964	12:22 am	Leo
11-05-1964	10:20 pm	Vir
06-28-1965	08:11 pm	Lib
08-20-1965	07:16 am	Sco
10-04-1965	01:47 am	Sag
11-14-1965	02:19 am	Cap
12-23-1965	12:37 am	Aqu
01-30-1966	02:02 am	Pis
03-09-1966	07:56 am	Ari

Date of Birth	Time of Birth	Mars Sign
04-17-1966	03:35 pm	Tau
05-28-1966	05:08 pm	Gem
07-10-1966	10:15 pm	Can
08-25-1966	10:52 am	Leo
10-12-1966	01:37 pm	Vir
12-03-1966	07:55 pm	Lib
02-12-1967	07:21 am	Sco
09-09-1967	08:44 pm	Sag
10-22-1967	09:15 pm	Cap
12-01-1967	03:12 pm	Aqu
01-09-1968	04:50 am	Pis
02-16-1968	10:18 pm	Ari
03-27-1968	06:43 pm	Tau
05-08-1968	09:15 am	Gem
06-21-1968	12:03 am	Can
08-05-1968	12:07 pm	Leo
09-21-1968	01:39 pm	Vir
11-09-1968	01:09 am	Lib
12-29-1968	05:07 pm	Sco
02-25-1969	01:21 am	Sag
09-21-1969	01:36 am	Cap
11-04-1969	01:51 pm	Aqu
12-15-1969	09:23 am	Pis
01-24-1970	04:30 pm	Ari
03-06-1970	08:28 pm	Tau
04-18-1970	01:59 pm	Gem
06-02-1970	01:50 am	Can

Date of Birth	Time of Birth	Mars Sign
07-18-1970	01:43 am	Leo
09-02-1970	11:57 pm	Vir
10-20-1970	05:57 am	Lib
12-06-1970	11:34 am	Sco
01-22-1971	08:34 pm	Sag
03-12-1971	05:11 am	Cap
05-03-1971	03:57 pm	Aqu
11-06-1971	07:33 am	Pis
12-26-1971	01:05 pm	Ari
02-10-1972	09:04 am	Tau
03-26-1972	11:30 pm	Gem
05-12-1972	08:14 am	Can
06-28-1972	11:09 am	Leo
08-14-1972	07:59 pm	Vir
09-30-1972	06:23 pm	Lib
11-15-1972	05:17 pm	Sco
12-30-1972	11:12 am	Sag
02-12-1973	12:51 am	Cap
03-26-1973	03:59 pm	Aqu
05-07-1973	11:10 pm	Pis
06-20-1973	03:54 pm	Ari
08-12-1973	09:55 am	Tau
02-27-1974	05:11 am	Gem
04-20-1974	03:18 am	Can
06-08-1974	07:54 pm	Leo
07-27-1974	09:05 am	Vir
09-12-1974	02:08 pm	Lib

Date of Birth	Time of Birth	Mars Sign
10-28-1974	02:05 am	Sco
12-10-1974	05:06 pm	Sag
01-21-1975	01:50 pm	Cap
03-03-1975	12:32 am	Aqu
04-11-1975	02:16 pm	Pis
05-21-1975	03:14 am	Ari
06-30-1975	10:53 pm	Tau
08-14-1975	03:47 pm	Gem
10-17-1975	03:43 am	Can
05-16-1976	06:11 am	Leo
07-06-1976	06:28 pm	Vir
08-24-1976	12:55 am	Lib
10-08-1976	03:24 pm	Sco
11-20-1976	06:54 pm	Sag
12-31-1976	07:42 pm	Cap
02-09-1977	06:57 am	Aqu
03-19-1977	09:20 pm	Pis
04-27-1977	10:47 am	Ari
06-05-1977	10:00 pm	Tau
07-17-1977	10:13 am	Gem
08-31-1977	07:20 pm	Can
10-26-1977	01:56 pm	Leo
06-13-1978	09:39 pm	Vir
08-04-1978	04:07 am	Lib
09-19-1978	03:57 pm	Sco
11-01-1978	08:21 pm	Sag
12-12-1978	12:39 pm	Cap

Date of Birth	Time of Birth	Mars Sign
01-20-1979	12:08 pm	Aqu
02-27-1979	03:26 pm	Pis
04-06-1979	08:09 pm	Ari
05-15-1979	11:25 pm	Tau
06-25-1979	08:56 pm	Gem
08-08-1979	08:29 am	Can
09-24-1979	04:22 pm	Leo
11-19-1979	04:37 pm	Vir
07-10-1980	12:58 pm	Lib
08-29-1980	12:51 pm	Sco
10-12-1980	01:27 am	Sag
11-21-1980	08:43 pm	Cap
12-30-1980	05:31 pm	Aqu
02-06-1981	05:49 pm	Pis
03-16-1981	09:41 pm	Ari
04-25-1981	02:17 pm	Tau
06-05-1981	12:27 pm	Gem
07-18-1981	03:55 pm	Can
09-01-1981	08:53 pm	Leo
10-20-1981	08:57 pm	Vir
12-15-1981	07:15 pm	Lib
08-03-1982	06:46 am	Sco
09-19-1982	08:20 pm	Sag
10-31-1982	06:05 pm	Cap
12-10-1982	01:17 am	Aqu
01-17-1983	08:11 am	Pis
02-24-1983	07:21 pm	Ari

Date of Birth	Time of Birth	Mars Sign
04-05-1983	09:04 am	Tau
05-16-1983	04:44 pm	Gem
06-29-1983	01:54 am	Can
08-13-1983	11:55 am	Leo
09-29-1983	07:12 pm	Vir
11-18-1983	05:26 am	Lib
01-10-1984	10:21 pm	Sco
08-17-1984	02:51 pm	Sag
10-05-1984	01:03 am	Cap
11-15-1984	01:09 pm	Aqu
12-25-1984	01:38 am	Pis
02-02-1985	12:20 pm	Ari
03-15-1985	12:07 am	Tau
04-26-1985	04:14 am	Gem
06-09-1985	05:41 am	Can
07-24-1985	11:05 pm	Leo
09-09-1985	08:32 pm	Vir
10-27-1985	10:16 am	Lib
12-14-1985	02:00 pm	Sco
02-02-1986	01:27 am	Sag
03-27-1986	10:46 pm	Cap
10-08-1986	08:01 pm	Aqu
11-25-1986	09:36 pm	Pis
01-08-1987	07:21 am	Ari
02-20-1987	09:44 am	Tau
04-05-1987	11:38 am	Gem
05-20-1987	10:01 pm	Can

Date of Birth	Time of Birth	Mars Sign
07-06-1987	11:47 am	Leo
08-22-1987	02:52 pm	Vir
10-08-1987	02:27 pm	Lib
11-23-1987	10:20 pm	Sco
01-08-1988	10:25 am	Sag
02-22-1988	05:16 am	Cap
04-06-1988	04:44 pm	Aqu
05-22-1988	02:42 am	Pis
07-13-1988	03:01 pm	Ari
01-19-1989	03:12 am	Tau
03-11-1989	03:52 am	Gem
04-28-1989	11:38 pm	Can
06-16-1989	09:11 am	Leo
08-03-1989	08:36 am	Vir
09-19-1989	09:38 am	Lib
11-04-1989	12:30 am	Sco
12-17-1989	11:57 pm	Sag
01-29-1990	09:12 am	Cap
03-11-1990	10:54 am	Aqu
04-20-1990	05:09 pm	Pis
05-31-1990	02:12 am	Ari
07-12-1990	09:44 am	Tau
08-31-1990	06:40 am	Gem
04-02-1991	07:49 pm	Can
05-26-1991	07:20 am	Leo
07-15-1991	07:37 am	Vir
09-01-1991	01:38 am	Lib

Date of Birth	Time of Birth	Mars Sign
10-16-1991	02:05 pm	Sco
11-28-1991	09:19 pm	Sag
01-09-1992	04:48 am	Cap
02-17-1992	11:38 pm	Aqu
03-27-1992	09:05 pm	Pis
05-05-1992	04:37 pm	Ari
06-14-1992	10:56 am	Tau
07-26-1992	02:00 pm	Gem
09-12-1992	01:05 am	Can
04-27-1993	06:41 pm	Leo
06-23-1993	02:43 am	Vir
08-11-1993	08:11 pm	Lib
09-26-1993	09:16 pm	Sco
11-09-1993	12:29 am	Sag
12-19-1993	07:35 pm	Cap
01-27-1994	11:06 pm	Aqu
03-07-1994	06:02 am	Pis
04-14-1994	01:02 pm	Ari
05-23-1994	05:37 pm	Tau
07-03-1994	05:31 pm	Gem
08-16-1994	02:16 pm	Can
10-04-1994	10:49 am	Leo
12-12-1994	06:29 am	Vir
07-21-1995	04:21 am	Lib
09-07-1995	02:01 am	Sco
10-20-1995	04:03 pm	Sag
11-30-1995	08:59 am	Cap

Date of Birth	Time of Birth	Mars Sign
01-08-1996	06:02 am	Aqu
02-15-1996	06:50 am	Pis
03-24-1996	10:13 am	Ari
05-02-1996	01:16 pm	Tau
06-12-1996	09:43 am	Gem
07-25-1996	01:33 pm	Can
09-09-1996	03:03 pm	Leo
10-30-1996	02:13 am	Vir
01-03-1997	03:10 am	Lib
08-14-1997	03:43 am	Sco
09-28-1997	05:23 pm	Sag
11-09-1997	12:34 am	Cap
12-18-1997	01:38 am	Aqu
01-25-1998	04:27 am	Pis
03-04-1998	11:19 am	Ari
04-12-1998	08:05 pm	Tau
05-23-1998	10:43 pm	Gem
07-06-1998	04:01 am	Can
08-20-1998	02:17 pm	Leo
10-07-1998	07:29 am	Vir
11-27-1998	05:11 am	Lib
01-26-1999	07:00 am	Sco
09-02-1999	02:30 pm	Sag
10-16-1999	08:36 pm	Cap
11-26-1999	01:57 am	Aqu
01-03-2000	0:01 pm	Pis
02-11-2000	08:05 pm	Ari

Date of Birth	Time of Birth	Mars Sign
03-22-2000	08:26 pm	Tau
05-03-2000	02:19 pm	Gem
06-16-2000	07:30 am	Can
07-31-2000	08:22 pm	Leo
09-16-2000	07:20 pm	Vir
11-03-2000	09:01 pm	Lib
12-23-2000	09:38 pm	Sco
02-14-2001	03:07 pm	Sag
09-08-2001	12:52 pm	Cap
10-27-2001	12:21 pm	Aqu
12-08-2001	04:53 pm	Pis
01-18-2002	05:54 pm	Ari
03-01-2002	10:05 am	Tau
04-13-2002	12:36 pm	Gem
05-28-2002	06:43 am	Can
07-13-2002	10:24 am	Leo
08-29-2002	09:38 am	Vir
10-15-2002	12:39 pm	Lib
12-01-2002	09:27 am	Sco
01-16-2003	11:23 pm	Sag
03-04-2003	04:18 pm	Cap
04-21-2003	06:48 pm	Aqu
06-16-2003	09:26 pm	Pis
12-16-2003	08:25 am	Ari
02-03-2004	05:06 am	Tau
03-21-2004	02:40 am	Gem
05-07-2004	03:46 am	Can

Date of Birth	Time of Birth	Mars Sign
06-23-2004	03:52 pm	Leo
08-10-2004	05:15 am	Vir
09-26-2004	04:16 am	Lib
11-11-2004	12:11 am	Sco
12-25-2004	11:05 am	Sag
02-06-2005	01:33 pm	Cap
03-20-2005	01:03 pm	Aqu
04-30-2005	09:58 pm	Pis
06-11-2005	09:31 pm	Ari
07-28-2005	12:13 am	Tau
02-17-2006	05:45 pm	Gem
04-13-2006	08:00 pm	Can
06-03-2006	01:44 pm	Leo
07-22-2006	01:53 pm	Vir
09-07-2006	11:19 pm	Lib
10-23-2006	11:38 am	Sco
12-05-2006	11:59 pm	Sag
01-16-2007	03:55 pm	Cap
02-25-2007	08:33 pm	Aqu
04-06-2007	03:50 am	Pis
05-15-2007	09:07 am	Ari
06-24-2007	04:27 pm	Tau
08-07-2007	01:02 am	Gem
09-28-2007	06:54 pm	Can
05-09-2008	03:21 pm	Leo
07-01-2008	11:21 am	Vir
08-19-2008	05:04 am	Lib

Date of Birth	Time of Birth	Mars Sign
10-03-2008	11:35 pm	Sco
11-16-2008	03:27 am	Sag
12-27-2008	02:31 am	Cap
02-04-2009	10:56 am	Aqu
03-14-2009	10:21 pm	Pis
04-22-2009	08:45 am	Ari
05-31-2009	04:19 pm	Tau
07-11-2009	09:57 pm	Gem
08-25-2009	12:16 pm	Can
10-16-2009	10:34 am	Leo
06-07-2010	01:12 am	Vir
07-29-2010	06:47 pm	Lib
09-14-2010	05:38 pm	Sco
10-28-2010	01:48 am	Sag
12-07-2010	06:50 pm	Cap
01-15-2011	05:42 pm	Aqu
02-22-2011	08:06 pm	Pis
04-01-2011	11:52 pm	Ari
05-11-2011	02:05 am	Tau
06-20-2011	09:51 pm	Gem
08-03-2011	04:23 am	Can
09-18-2011	08:51 pm	Leo
11-10-2011	11:15 pm	Vir
07-03-2012	07:33 am	Lib
08-23-2012	10:25 am	Sco
10-06-2012	10:21 pm	Sag
11-16-2012	09:37 pm	Cap

Date of Birth	Time of Birth	Mars Sign
12-25-2012	07:49 pm	Aqu
02-01-2013	08:54 pm	Pis
03-12-2013	01:27 am	Ari
04-20-2013	06:49 am	Tau
05-31-2013	05:40 am	Gem
07-13-2013	08:23 am	Can
08-27-2013	09:05 pm	Leo
10-15-2013	06:06 am	Vir
12-07-2013	03:42 pm	Lib
07-25-2014	09:26 pm	Sco
09-13-2014	04:58 pm	Sag
10-26-2014	5:43 am	Cap
12-04-2014	06:57 pm	Aqu
01-12-2015	05:21 am	Pis
02-19-2015	07:12 pm	Ari
03-31-2015	11:27 am	Tau
05-11-2015	09:41 pm	Gem
06-24-2015	08:34 am	Can
08-08-2015	06:33 pm	Leo
09-24-2015	09:19 pm	Vir
11-12-2015	04:42 pm	Lib

VENUS SIGN POSITIONS 1930–2015

Date of Birth	Time of Birth	Venus Sign
01-23-1930	07:22 pm	Aqu
02-16-1930	05:11 pm	Pis
03-12-1930	05:34 pm	Ari
04-05-1930	09:57 pm	Tau
04-30-1930	07:37 am	Gem
05-24-1930	11:36 pm	Can
06-18-1930	11:39 pm	Leo
07-14-1930	11:34 am	Vir
08-09-1930	07:54 pm	Lib
09-06-1930	11:05 pm	Sco
10-11-1930	09:45 pm	Sag
02-06-1931	07:25 am	Cap
03-05-1931	04:46 pm	Aqu
03-31-1931	02:04 pm	Pis
04-25-1931	09:10 pm	Ari
05-20-1931	09:38 pm	Tau
06-14-1931	06:04 pm	Gem
07-09-1931	10:35 am	Can
08-02-1931	10:29 pm	Leo
08-27-1931	05:42 am	Vir
09-20-1931	09:15 am	Lib
10-14-1931	10:45 am	Sco
11-07-1931	11:32 am	Sag
12-01-1931	12:29 pm	Cap
12-25-1931	02:44 pm	Aqu
01-18-1932	08:52 pm	Pis

Date of Birth	Time of Birth	Venus Sign
02-12-1932	11:58 am	Ari
03-08-1932	09:07 pm	Tau
04-04-1932	07:19 pm	Gem
05-06-1932	04:04 am	Can
09-08-1932	02:45 pm	Leo
10-07-1932	12:46 am	Vir
11-01-1932	11:01 pm	Lib
11-26-1932	07:06 pm	Sco
12-21-1932	02:43 am	Sag
01-14-1933	04:56 am	Cap
02-07-1933	05:30 am	Aqu
03-03-1933	06:25 am	Pis
03-27-1933	08:58 am	Ari
04-20-1933	02:00 pm	Tau
05-14-1933	09:47 pm	Gem
06-08-1933	08:01 am	Can
07-02-1933	08:2 pm	Leo
07-27-1933	11:45 am	Vir
08-21-1933	07:23 am	Lib
09-15-1933	09:54 am	Sco
10-10-1933	11:32 pm	Sag
11-06-1933	11:02 am	Cap
12-05-1933	01:00 pm	Aqu
04-06-1934	04:23 am	Pis
05-06-1934	03:54 am	Ari
06-02-1934	05:11 am	Tau
06-28-1934	04:38 am	Gem

Date of Birth	Time of Birth	Venus Sign
07-23-1934	01:22 pm	Can
08-17-1934	10:45 am	Leo
09-10-1934	10:32 pm	Vir
10-05-1934	02:56 am	Lib
10-29-1934	02:37 am	Sco
11-21-1934	11:59 pm	Sag
12-15-1934	08:39 pm	Cap
01-08-1935	05:44 pm	Aqu
02-01-1935	04:36 pm	Pis
02-25-1935	07:30 pm	Ari
03-22-1935	05:29 am	Tau
04-16-1935	02:37 am	Gem
05-11-1935	05:01 pm	Can
06-07-1935	02:11 pm	Leo
07-07-1935	03:33 pm	Vir
11-09-1935	11:34 am	Lib
12-08-1935	09:36 am	Sco
01-03-1936	09:16 am	Sag
01-28-1936	09:00 am	Cap
02-21-1936	11:14 pm	Aqu
03-17-1936	09:53 am	Pis
04-10-1936	07:41 am	Ari
05-05-1936	05:53 am	Tau
05-29-1936	04:39 pm	Gem
06-23-1936	03:16 am	Can
07-17-1936	12:51 pm	Leo
08-10-1936	09:11pm	Vir

Date of Birth	Time of Birth	Venus Sign
09-04-1936	05:02am	Lib
09-28-1936	01:36pm	Sco
10-23-1936	12:00am	Sag
11-16-1936	01:36pm	Cap
12-11-1936	09:51am	Aqu
01-05-1937	10:18pm	Pis
02-02-1937	05:39 am	Ari
03-09-1937	08:19 am	Tau
07-07-1937	04:13 pm	Gem
08-04-1937	03:14 pm	Can
08-30-1937	07:08 pm	Leo
09-24-1937	11:03 pm	Vir
10-19-1937	11:33 am	Lib
11-12-1937	02:43 pm	Sco
12-06-1937	01:06 pm	Sag
12-30-1937	09:42 am	Cap
01-23-1938	06:16 am	Aqu
02-16-1938	04:00 am	Pis
03-12-1938	04:20 am	Ari
04-05-1938	08:46 am	Tau
04-29-1938	06:35 pm	Gem
05-24-1938	10:56 am	Can
06-18-1938	11:37 am	Leo
07-14-1938	12:45 am	Vir
08-09-1938	11:27 am	Lib
09-06-1938	08:36 pm	Sco
10-13-1938	01:49 pm	Sag

Date of Birth	Time of Birth	Venus Sign
02-06-1939	04:20am	Cap
03-05-1939	08:29 am	Aqu
03-31-1939	03:34 am	Pis
04-25-1939	09:28 am	Ari
05-20-1939	09:13 am	Tau
06-14-1939	05:11 am	Gem
07-08-1939	09:25 pm	Can
08-02-1939	09:12 am	Leo
08-26-1939	04:24 pm	Vir
09-19-1939	08:02 pm	Lib
10-13-1939	09:41 pm	Sco
11-06-1939	10:41 pm	Sag
11-30-1939	11:52 pm	Cap
12-25-1939	02:25 am	Aqu
01-18-1940	09:00 am	Pis
02-12-1940	12:51 am	Ari
03-08-1940	11:25 am	Tau
04-04-1940	01:10 pm	Gem
05-06-1940	01:47 pm	Can
09-08-1940	11:59 am	Leo
10-06-1940	04:10 pm	Vir
11-01-1940	12:24 pm	Lib
11-26-1940	07:32 am	Sco
12-20-1940	02:36 pm	Sag
01-13-1941	04:29 pm	Cap
02-06-1941	04:49 pm	Aqu
03-02-1941	05:33 pm	Pis

Date of Birth	Time of Birth	Venus Sign
03-26-1941	07:58 pm	Ari
04-20-1941	12:53 am	Tau
05-14-1941	08:36 am	Gem
06-07-1941	06:53 pm	Can
07-02-1941	07:33 am	Leo
07-26-1941	11:12 pm	Vir
08-20-1941	07:29 pm	Lib
09-14-1941	11:01 pm	Sco
10-10-1941	02:22 pm	Sag
11-06-1941	05:17 am	Cap
12-05-1941	06:04 pm	Aqu
04-06-1942	08:14 am	Pis
05-05-1942	09:26 pm	Ari
06-01-1942	07:26 pm	Tau
06-27-1942	05:18 pm	Gem
07-23-1942	01:10 am	Can
08-16-1942	10:04 pm	Leo
09-10-1942	09:38 am	Vir
10-04-1942	01:58 pm	Lib
10-28-1942	01:41 pm	Sco
11-21-1942	11:07 pm	Sag
12-15-1942	07:53 am	Cap
01-08-1943	05:03 am	Aqu
02-01-1943	04:02 am	Pis
02-25-1943	07:05 am	Ari
03-21-1943	05:24 pm	Tau
04-15-1943	03:12 pm	Gem

Date of Birth	Time of Birth	Venus Sign
05-11-1943	06:57 am	Can
06-07-1943	07:09 am	Leo
07-07-1943	06:56 pm	Vir
11-09-1943	01:25 pm	Lib
12-08-1943	02:45 am	Sco
01-02-1944	11:44 pm	Sag
01-27-1944	10:11 pm	Cap
02-21-1944	11:40 am	Aqu
03-16-1944	09:47 pm	Pis
04-10-1944	07:09 am	Ari
05-04-1944	05:04 pm	Tau
05-29-1944	03:39 am	Gem
06-22-1944	02:12 pm	Can
07-16-1944	11:47 pm	Leo
08-10-1944	08:13 am	Vir
09-03-1944	04:17 pm	Lib
09-28-1944	01:12 am	Sco
10-22-1944	12:07 pm	Sag
11-16-1944	02:26 am	Cap
12-10-1944	11:47 pm	Aqu
01-05-1945	02:18 pm	Pis
02-02-1945	03:07 am	Ari
03-11-1945	06:17 am	Tau
07-07-1945	11:20 am	Gem
08-04-1945	05:59 am	Can
08-30-1945	08:05 am	Leo
09-24-1945	11:07 am	Vir

Date of Birth	Time of Birth	Venus Sign
10-18-1945	11:09 pm	Lib
11-12-1945	02:05 am	Sco
12-06-1945	12:22 am	Sag
12-29-1945	08:56 pm	Cap
01-22-1946	05:28 pm	Aqu
02-15-1946	03:11 pm	Pis
03-11-1946	03:32 pm	Ari
04-04-1946	08:01 pm	Tau
04-29-1946	05:59 am	Gem
05-23-1946	10:40 pm	Can
06-18-1946	12:00 am	Leo
07-13-1946	02:22 pm	Vir
08-09-1946	03:34 am	Lib
09-06-1946	07:16 pm	Sco
10-16-1946	05:45 am	Sag
02-06-1947	12:41 am	Cap
03-05-1947	12:09 am	Aqu
03-30-1947	05:15 pm	Pis
04-24-1947	10:03 pm	Ari
05-19-1947	09:06 pm	Tau
06-13-1947	04:35 pm	Gem
07-08-1947	08:30 am	Can
08-01-1947	08:06 pm	Leo
08-26-1947	03:17 am	Vir
09-19-1947	07:01 am	Lib
10-13-1947	08:49 am	Sco
11-06-1947	09:59 am	Sag

Date of Birth	Time of Birth	Venus Sign
11-30-1947	11:23 am	Cap
12-24-1947	02:13 pm	Aqu
01-17-1948	09:14 pm	Pis
02-11-1948	01:51 pm	Ari
03-08-1948	01:59 am	Tau
04-04-1948	07:40 am	Gem
05-07-1948	03:28 am	Can
09-08-1948	08:41 am	Leo
10-06-1948	07:25 am	Vir
11-01-1948	01:42 am	Lib
11-25-1948	07:55 pm	Sco
12-20-1948	02:28 am	Sag
01-13-1949	04:01 am	Cap
02-06-1949	04:06 am	Aqu
03-02-1949	04:38 am	Pis
03-26-1949	06:54 am	Ari
04-19-1949	11:44 am	Tau
05-13-1949	07:26 pm	Gem
06-07-1949	05:47 am	Can
07-01-1949	06:41 pm	Leo
07-26-1949	10:44 am	Vir
08-20-1949	07:39 am	Lib
09-14-1949	12:12 pm	Sco
10-10-1949	05:18 am	Sag
11-05-1949	11:53 pm	Cap
12-06-1949	01:06 am	Aqu
04-06-1950	10:14 am	Pis

Date of Birth	Time of Birth	Venus Sign
05-05-1950	02:19 pm	Ari
06-01-1950	09:19 am	Tau
06-27-1950	05:45 am	Gem
07-22-1950	12:50 pm	Can
08-16-1950	09:18 am	Leo
09-09-1950	08:37 pm	Vir
10-04-1950	12:51 am	Lib
10-28-1950	12:33 am	Sco
11-20-1950	10:03 pm	Sag
12-14-1950	06:54 pm	Cap
01-07-1951	04:10 pm	Aqu
01-31-1951	03:15 pm	Pis
02-24-1951	06:27 pm	Ari
03-21-1951	05:06 am	Tau
04-15-1951	03:33 am	Gem
05-10-1951	08:42 pm	Can
06-07-1951	12:10 am	Leo
07-07-1951	11:54 pm	Vir
11-09-1951	01:48 pm	Lib
12-07-1951	07:19 pm	Sco
01-02-1952	01:44 pm	Sag
01-27-1952	10:58 am	Cap
02-20-1952	11:43 pm	Aqu
03-16-1952	09:18 am	Pis
04-09-1952	06:18 pm	Ari
05-04-1952	03:55 am	Tau
05-28-1952	02:19 pm	Gem

Date of Birth	Time of Birth	Venus Sign
06-22-1952	12:46 am	Can
07-16-1952	10:23 am	Leo
08-09-1952	06:58 pm	Vir
09-03-1952	03:17 am	Lib
09-27-1952	12:36 pm	Sco
10-22-1952	12:02 am	Sag
11-15-1952	03:03 pm	Cap
12-10-1952	01:31 pm	Aqu
01-05-1953	06:11 am	Pis
02-02-1953	12:54 am	Ari
03-14-1953	01:58 pm	Tau
07-07-1953	05:30 am	Gem
08-03-1953	08:09 pm	Can
08-29-1953	08:35 pm	Leo
09-23-1953	10:48 pm	Vir
10-18-1953	10:27 am	Lib
11-11-1953	01:12 pm	Sco
12-05-1953	11:24 am	Sag
12-29-1953	07:54 am	Cap
01-22-1954	04:21 am	Aqu
02-15-1954	02:01 am	Pis
03-11-1954	02:22 am	Ari
04-04-1954	06:55 am	Tau
04-28-1954	05:03 pm	Gem
05-23-1954	10:04 am	Can
06-17-1954	12:04 pm	Leo
07-13-1954	03:43 am	Vir

Date of Birth	Time of Birth	Venus Sign
08-08-1954	07:34 pm	Lib
09-06-1954	06:29 pm	Sco
10-23-1954	05:06 pm	Sag
02-05-1955	08:16 pm	Cap
03-04-1955	03:22 pm	Aqu
03-30-1955	06:30 pm	Pis
04-24-1955	10:13 am	Ari
05-19-1955	08:35 am	Tau
06-13-1955	03:38 am	Gem
07-07-1955	07:15 pm	Can
08-01-1955	06:43 am	Leo
08-25-1955	01:52 pm	Vir
09-18-1955	05:41 pm	Lib
10-12-1955	07:39 pm	Sco
11-05-1955	09:02 pm	Sag
11-29-1955	10:42 pm	Cap
12-24-1955	01:53 am	Aqu
01-17-1956	09:22 am	Pis
02-11-1956	02:47 am	Ari
03-07-1956	04:32 pm	Tau
04-04-1956	02:23 am	Gem
05-07-1956	09:17 pm	Can
09-08-1956	04:24 am	Leo
10-05-1956	10:12 pm	Vir
10-31-1956	02:40 pm	Lib
11-25-1956	08:01 am	Sco
12-19-1956	02:07 pm	Sag

Date of Birth	Time of Birth	Venus Sign
01-12-1957	03:23 pm	Cap
02-05-1957	03:16 pm	Aqu
03-01-1957	03:39 pm	Pis
03-25-1957	05:46 pm	Ari
04-18-1957	10:29 pm	Tau
05-13-1957	06:08 am	Gem
06-06-1957	04:35 pm	Can
07-01-1957	05:42 am	Leo
07-25-1957	10:10 pm	Vir
08-19-1957	07:44 pm	Lib
09-14-1957	01:20 am	Sco
10-09-1957	08:16 pm	Sag
11-05-1957	06:46 pm	Cap
12-06-1957	10:26 am	Aqu
04-06-1958	11:00 am	Pis
05-05-1958	06:59 am	Ari
05-31-1958	11:07 pm	Tau
06-26-1958	06:08 pm	Gem
07-22-1958	12:26 am	Can
08-15-1958	08:28 pm	Leo
09-09-1958	07:35 am	Vir
10-03-1958	11:44 am	Lib
10-27-1958	11:26 am	Sco
11-20-1958	08:59 am	Sag
12-14-1958	05:55 am	Cap
01-07-1959	03:17 am	Aqu
01-31-1959	02:28 am	Pis

Date of Birth	Time of Birth	Venus Sign
02-24-1959	05:53 am	Ari
03-20-1959	04:56 pm	Tau
04-14-1959	04:08 pm	Gem
05-10-1959	10:45 am	Can
06-06-1959	05:43 pm	Leo
07-08-1959	07:08 am	Vir
11-09-1959	01:11 pm	Lib
12-07-1959	11:42 am	Sco
01-02-1960	03:43 am	Sag
01-26-1960	11:46 pm	Cap
02-20-1960	11:47 am	Aqu
03-15-1960	08:54 pm	Pis
04-09-1960	05:32 am	Ari
05-03-1960	02:56 pm	Tau
05-28-1960	01:11 am	Gem
06-21-1960	11:34 am	Can
07-15-1960	09:11 pm	Leo
08-09-1960	05:54 am	Vir
09-02-1960	02:30 pm	Lib
09-27-1960	12:13 am	Sco
10-21-1960	12:12 pm	Sag
11-15-1960	03:57 am	Cap
12-10-1960	03:34 am	Aqu
01-04-1961	10:31 pm	Pis
02-01-1961	11:46 pm	Ari
06-05-1961	02:25 pm	Tau
07-06-1961	11:32 pm	Gem

Date of Birth	Time of Birth	Venus Sign
08-03-1961	10:28 am	Can
08-29-1961	09:18 am	Leo
09-23-1961	10:43 am	Vir
10-17-1961	09:58 pm	Lib
11-11-1961	12:33 am	Sco
12-04-1961	10:40 pm	Sag
12-28-1961	07:07 pm	Cap
01-21-1962	03:31 pm	Aqu
02-14-1962	01:09 pm	Pis
03-10-1962	01:29 pm	Ari
04-03-1962	06:05 pm	Tau
04-28-1962	04:23 pm	Gem
05-22-1962	09:46 pm	Can
06-17-1962	12:31 pm	Leo
07-12-1962	05:32 pm	Vir
08-08-1962	12:14 pm	Lib
09-06-1962	07:11 pm	Sco
01-06-1963	12:35 pm	Sag
02-05-1963	03:36 pm	Cap
03-04-1963	06:42 am	Aqu
03-29-1963	08:00 pm	Pis
04-23-1963	10:40 pm	Ari
05-18-1963	08:21 pm	Tau
06-12-1963	02:57 pm	Gem
07-07-1963	06:18 am	Can
07-31-1963	05:39 pm	Leo
08-25-1963	12:49 am	Vir

Date of Birth	Time of Birth	Venus Sign
09-18-1963	04:43 am	Lib
10-12-1963	06:50 am	Sco
11-05-1963	08:25 am	Sag
11-29-1963	10:21 am	Cap
12-23-1963	01:53 pm	Aqu
01-16-1964	09:54 pm	Pis
02-10-1964	04:10 pm	Ari
03-07-1964	07:38 am	Tau
04-03-1964	10:03 pm	Gem
05-08-1964	10:16 pm	Can
09-07-1964	11:53 pm	Leo
10-05-1964	01:10 pm	Vir
10-31-1964	03:54 am	Lib
11-24-1964	08:25 pm	Sco
12-19-1964	02:02 am	Sag
01-12-1965	03:01 am	Cap
02-05-1965	02:42 am	Aqu
03-01-1965	02:55 am	Pis
03-25-1965	04:54 am	Ari
04-18-1965	09:31 am	Tau
05-12-1965	05:08 pm	Gem
06-06-1965	03:39 am	Can
06-30-1965	04:59 pm	Leo
07-25-1965	09:52 am	Vir
08-19-1965	08:07 am	Lib
09-13-1965	02:50 pm	Sco
10-09-1965	11:46 am	Sag

Date of Birth	Time of Birth	Venus Sign
11-05-1965	02:36 pm	Cap
12-06-1965	11:37 pm	Aqu
04-06-1966	10:54 am	Pis
05-04-1966	11:34 pm	Ari
05-31-1966	01:01 pm	Tau
06-26-1966	06:40 am	Gem
07-21-1966	12:12 pm	Can
08-15-1966	07:48 am	Leo
09-08-1966	06:41 pm	Vir
10-02-1966	10:44 pm	Lib
10-26-1966	10:28 pm	Sco
11-19-1966	08:07 pm	Sag
12-13-1966	05:09 pm	Cap
01-06-1967	02:36 pm	Aqu
01-30-1967	01:54 pm	Pis
02-23-1967	05:30 pm	Ari
03-20-1967	04:56 am	Tau
04-14-1967	04:55 am	Gem
05-10-1967	01:05 am	Can
06-06-1967	11:48 am	Leo
07-08-1967	05:12 pm	Vir
11-09-1967	11:32 am	Lib
12-07-1967	03:48 am	Sco
01-01-1968	05:38 pm	Sag
01-26-1968	12:35 pm	Cap
02-19-1968	11:55 pm	Aqu
03-15-1968	08:32 am	Pis

Date of Birth	Time of Birth	Venus Sign
04-08-1968	04:49 pm	Ari
05-03-1968	01:57 am	Tau
05-27-1968	12:02 pm	Gem
06-20-1968	10:21 pm	Can
07-15-1968	07:59 am	Leo
08-08-1968	04:49 pm	Vir
09-02-1968	01:40 am	Lib
09-26-1968	11:46 am	Sco
10-21-1968	12:17 am	Sag
11-14-1968	04:48 pm	Cap
12-09-1968	05:40 pm	Aqu
01-04-1969	03:07 pm	Pis
02-01-1969	11:45 pm	Ari
06-05-1969	08:49 pm	Tau
07-06-1969	05:04 pm	Gem
08-03-1969	12:30 am	Can
08-28-1969	09:48 pm	Leo
09-22-1969	10:26 pm	Vir
10-17-1969	09:18 am	Lib
11-10-1969	11:40 am	Sco
12-04-1969	09:41 am	Sag
12-28-1969	06:04 am	Cap
01-21-1970	02:26 am	Aqu
02-14-1970	12:04 am	Pis
03-10-1970	12:25 am	Ari
04-03-1970	05:05 am	Tau
04-27-1970	03:33 pm	Gem

Date of Birth	Time of Birth	Venus Sign
05-22-1970	09:20 am	Can
06-16-1970	12:49 pm	Leo
07-12-1970	07:17 am	Vir
08-08-1970	05:00 am	Lib
09-06-1970	08:54 pm	Sco
01-06-1971	08:00 pm	Sag
02-05-1971	09:57 am	Cap
03-03-1971	09:24 pm	Aqu
03-29-1971	09:02 am	Pis
04-23-1971	10:44 am	Ari
05-18-1971	07:48 am	Tau
06-12-1971	01:58 am	Gem
07-06-1971	05:03 pm	Can
07-31-1971	04:15 am	Leo
08-24-1971	11:25 am	Vir
09-17-1971	03:26 pm	Lib
10-11-1971	05:43 pm	Sco
11-04-1971	07:31 pm	Sag
11-28-1971	09:42 pm	Cap
12-23-1971	01:33 am	Aqu
01-16-1972	10:02 am	Pis
02-10-1972	05:09 am	Ari
03-06-1972	10:26 pm	Tau
04-03-1972	05:48 pm	Gem
05-10-1972	08:51 am	Can
09-07-1972	06:27 pm	Leo
10-05-1972	03:34 am	Vir

Date of Birth	Time of Birth	Venus Sign
10-30-1972	04:40 pm	Lib
11-24-1972	08:24 am	Sco
12-18-1972	01:34 pm	Sag
01-11-1973	02:15 pm	Cap
02-04-1973	01:43 pm	Aqu
02-28-1973	01:45 pm	Pis
03-24-1973	03:35 pm	Ari
04-17-1973	08:05 pm	Tau
05-12-1973	03:43 am	Gem
06-05-1973	02:20 pm	Can
06-30-1973	03:55 am	Leo
07-24-1973	09:13 pm	Vir
08-18-1973	08:11 pm	Lib
09-13-1973	04:05 am	Sco
10-09-1973	03:08 am	Sag
11-05-1973	10:40 am	Cap
12-07-1973	04:38 pm	Aqu
04-06-1974	09:17 am	Pis
05-04-1974	03:22 pm	Ari
05-31-1974	02:19 am	Tau
06-25-1974	06:44 pm	Gem
07-20-1974	11:34 pm	Can
08-14-1974	06:47 pm	Leo
09-08-1974	05:28 am	Vir
10-02-1974	09:27 am	Lib
10-26-1974	09:13 am	Sco
11-19-1974	06:57 am	Sag

Date of Birth	Time of Birth	Venus Sign
12-13-1974	04:06 am	Cap
01-06-1975	01:40 am	Aqu
01-30-1975	01:05 am	Pis
02-23-1975	04:53 am	Ari
03-19-1975	04:42 pm	Tau
04-13-1975	05:26 pm	Gem
05-09-1975	03:12 pm	Can
06-06-1975	05:55 am	Leo
07-09-1975	06:07 am	Vir
11-09-1975	08:52 am	Lib
12-06-1975	07:29 pm	Sco
01-01-1976	07:15 am	Sag
01-26-1976	01:09 am	Cap
02-19-1976	11:51 am	Aqu
03-14-1976	08:00 pm	Pis
04-08-1976	03:56 am	Ari
05-02-1976	12:49 pm	Tau
05-26-1976	10:44 pm	Gem
06-20-1976	08:56 am	Can
07-14-1976	06:36 pm	Leo
08-08-1976	03:36 am	Vir
09-01-1976	12:45 pm	Lib
09-25-1976	11:17 pm	Sco
10-20-1976	12:23 pm	Sag
11-14-1976	05:42 am	Cap
12-09-1976	07:53 am	Aqu
01-04-1977	08:02 am	Pis

Date of Birth	Time of Birth	Venus Sign
02-02-1977	12:55 am	Ari
06-06-1977	01:11 am	Tau
07-06-1977	10:09 am	Gem
08-02-1977	02:19 pm	Can
08-28-1977	10:10 am	Leo
09-22-1977	10:06 am	Vir
10-16-1977	08:38 pm	Lib
11-09-1977	10:52 pm	Sco
12-03-1977	08:49 pm	Sag
12-27-1977	05:10 pm	Cap
01-20-1978	01:30 pm	Aqu
02-13-1978	11:07 am	Pis
03-09-1978	11:29 am	Ari
04-02-1978	04:14 pm	Tau
04-27-1978	02:54 am	Gem
05-21-1978	09:04 pm	Can
06-16-1978	01:19 am	Leo
07-11-1978	09:14 pm	Vir
08-07-1978	10:09 pm	Lib
09-07-1978	12:08 am	Sco
01-07-1979	01:38 am	Sag
02-05-1979	04:16 am	Cap
03-03-1979	12:19 pm	Aqu
03-28-1979	10:18 pm	Pis
04-22-1979	11:03 pm	Ari
05-17-1979	07:29 pm	Tau
06-11-1979	01:14 pm	Gem

Date of Birth	Time of Birth	Venus Sign
07-06-1979	04:03 am	Can
07-30-1979	03:07 pm	Leo
08-23-1979	10:17 pm	Vir
09-17-1979	02:22 am	Lib
10-11-1979	04:48 am	Sco
11-04-1979	06:50 am	Sag
11-28-1979	09:20 am	Cap
12-22-1979	01:35 pm	Aqu
01-15-1980	10:37 pm	Pis
02-09-1980	06:40 pm	Ari
03-06-1980	01:55 pm	Tau
04-03-1980	02:47 pm	Gem
05-12-1980	03:53 pm	Can
09-07-1980	12:58 pm	Leo
10-04-1980	06:07 pm	Vir
10-30-1980 pm	05:38 am	Lib
11-23-1980	08:35 pm	Sco
12-18-1980	01:21 am	Sag
01-11-1981	01:49 am	Cap
02-04-1981	01:08 am	Aqu
02-28-1981	01:02 am	Pis
03-24-1981	02:43 am	Ari
04-17-1981	07:09 am	Tau
05-11-1981	02:45 pm	Gem
06-05-1981	01:30 am	Can
06-29-1981	03:20 pm	Leo
07-24-1981	09:04 am	Vir

Date of Birth	Time of Birth	Venus Sign
08-18-1981	08:45 am	Lib
09-12-1981	05:51 pm	Sco
10-08-1981	07:05 pm	Sag
11-05-1981	07:40 am	Cap
12-08-1981	03:53 pm	Aqu
04-06-1982	07:21 am	Pis
05-04-1982	07:27 am	Ari
05-30-1982	04:02 pm	Tau
06-25-1982	07:13 am	Gem
07-20-1982	11:21 am	Can
08-14-1982	06:10 am	Leo
09-07-1982	04:38 pm	Vir
10-01-1982	08:33 pm	Lib
10-25-1982	08:19 pm	Sco
11-18-1982	06:07 pm	Sag
12-12-1982	03:20 pm	Cap
01-05-1983	12:59 pm	Aqu
01-29-1983	12:32 pm	Pis
02-22-1983	04:35 pm	Ari
03-19-1983	04:52 am	Tau
04-13-1983	06:26 am	Gem
05-09-1983	05:57 am	Can
06-06-1983	01:04 am	Leo
07-10-1983	12:25 am	Vir
11-09-1983	05:53 am	Lib
12-06-1983	11:15 am	Sco
12-31-1983	09:01 pm	Sag

Date of Birth	Time of Birth	Venus Sign
01-25-1984	01:51 pm	Cap
02-18-1984	11:53 pm	Aqu
03-14-1984	07:35 am	Pis
04-07-1984	03:14 pm	Ari
05-01-1984	11:54 pm	Tau
05-26-1984	09:40 am	Gem
06-19-1984	07:49 pm	Can
07-14-1984	05:31 am	Leo
08-07-1984	02:40 pm	Vir
09-01-1984	12:07 am	Lib
09-25-1984	11:06 am	Sco
10-20-1984	12:46 am	Sag
11-13-1984	06:55 pm	Cap
12-08-1984	10:27 pm	Aqu
01-04-1985	01:24 am	Pis
02-02-1985	03:29 am	Ari
06-06-1985	03:53 am	Tau
07-06-1985	03:02 am	Gem
08-02-1985	04:11 am	Can
08-27-1985	10:39 pm	Leo
09-21-1985	09:53 pm	Vir
10-16-1985	08:04 am	Lib
11-09-1985	10:08 am	Sco
12-03-1985	08:00 am	Sag
12-27-1985	04:18 am	Cap
01-20-1986	12:36 am	Aqu
02-12-1986	10:11 pm	Pis

Date of Birth	Time of Birth	Venus Sign
03-08-1986	10:32 pm	Ari
04-02-1986	03:20 am	Tau
04-26-1986	02:11 pm	Gem
05-21-1986	08:46 am	Can
06-15-1986	01:52 pm	Leo
07-11-1986	11:23 am	Vir
08-07-1986	03:46 pm	Lib
09-07-1986	05:16 am	Sco
01-07-1987	05:20 am	Sag
02-04-1987	10:04 pm	Cap
03-03-1987	02:56 am	Aqu
03-28-1987	11:20 am	Pis
04-22-1987	11:08 am	Ari
05-17-1987	06:56 am	Tau
06-11-1987	12:16 am	Gem
07-05-1987	02:50 pm	Can
07-30-1987	01:50 am	Leo
08-23-1987	09:01 am	Vir
09-16-1987	01:12 pm	Lib
10-10-1987	03:49 pm	Sco
11-03-1987	06:05 pm	Sag
11-27-1987	08:52 pm	Cap
12-22-1987	01:29 am	Aqu
01-15-1988	11:04 am	Pis
02-09-1988	08:04 am	Ari
03-06-1988	05:21 am	Tau
04-03-1988	12:08 pm	Gem

Date of Birth	Time of Birth	Venus Sign
05-17-1988	11:27 am	Can
09-07-1988	06:38 am	Leo
10-04-1988	08:15 am	Vir
10-29-1988	06:20 pm	Lib
11-23-1988	08:34 am	Sco
12-17-1988	12:56 pm	Sag
01-10-1989	01:08 pm	Cap
02-03-1989	12:16 pm	Aqu
02-27-1989	11:59 am	Pis
03-23-1989	01:33 pm	Ari
04-16-1989	05:53 pm	Tau
05-11-1989	01:29 am	Gem
06-04-1989	12:18 pm	Can
06-29-1989	02:22 am	Leo
07-23-1989	08:32 pm	Vir
08-17-1989	08:58 pm	Lib
09-12-1989	07:23 am	Sco
10-08-1989	11:00 am	Sag
11-05-1989	05:14 am	Cap
12-09-1989	11:55 pm	Aqu
04-06-1990	04:14 am	Pis
05-03-1990	10:53 pm	Ari
05-30-1990	05:14 am	Tau
06-24-1990	07:15 pm	Gem
07-19-1990	10:41 pm	Can
08-13-1990	05:05 pm	Leo
09-07-1990	03:21 am	Vir

Date of Birth	Time of Birth	Venus Sign
10-01-1990	07:13 am	Lib
10-25-1990	07:04 am	Sco
11-18-1990	04:59 am	Sag
12-12-1990	02:19 am	Cap
01-05-1991	12:04 am	Aqu
01-28-1991	11:45 pm	Pis
02-22-1991	04:02 am	Ari
03-18-1991	04:45 pm	Tau
04-12-1991	07:11 pm	Gem
05-08-1991	08:29 pm	Can
06-05-1991	08:17 pm	Leo
10-06-1991	04:16 pm	Vir
11-09-1991	01:37 am	Lib
12-06-1991	02:22 am	Sco
12-31-1991	10:20 am	Sag
01-25-1992	02:15 am	Cap
02-18-1992	11:41 am	Aqu
03-13-1992	06:57 pm	Pis
04-07-1992	02:16 am	Ari
05-01-1992	10:42 am	Tau
05-25-1992	08:18 pm	Gem
06-19-1992	06:23 am	Can
07-13-1992	04:07 pm	Leo
08-07-1992	01:26 am	Vir
08-31-1992	11:09 am	Lib
09-24-1992	10:32 pm	Sco
10-19-1992	12:47 pm	Sag

Date of Birth	Time of Birth	Venus Sign
11-13-1992	07:49 am	Cap
12-08-1992	12:50 pm	Aqu
01-03-1993	06:54 pm	Pis
02-02-1993	07:38 am	Ari
06-06-1993	05:04 am	Tau
07-05-1993	07:22 pm	Gem
08-01-1993	05:39 pm	Can
08-27-1993	10:49 am	Leo
09-21-1993	09:23 am	Vir
10-15-1993	07:13 pm	Lib
11-08-1993	09:07 pm	Sco
12-02-1993	06:54 pm	Sag
12-26-1993	03:10 pm	Cap
01-19-1994	11:28 am	Aqu
02-12-1994	09:05 am	Pis
03-08-1994	09:28 am	Ari
04-01-1994	02:21 pm	Tau
04-26-1994	01:24 am	Gem
05-20-1994	08:27 pm	Can
06-15-1994	02:24 am	Leo
07-11-1994	01:34 am	Vir
08-07-1994	09:37 am	Lib
09-07-1994	12:13 pm	Sco
01-07-1995	07:07 am	Sag
02-04-1995	03:12 pm	Cap
03-02-1995	05:11 pm	Aqu
03-28-1995	12:11 am	Pis

Date of Birth	Time of Birth	Venus Sign
04-21-1995	11:08 pm	Ari
05-16-1995	06:23 pm	Tau
06-10-1995	11:19 am	Gem
07-05-1995	01:39 am	Can
07-29-1995	12:32 pm	Leo
08-22-1995	07:44 pm	Vir
09-16-1995	12:01 am	Lib
10-10-1995	02:49 am	Sco
11-03-1995	05:19 am	Sag
11-27-1995	08:24 am	Cap
12-21-1995	01:24 pm	Aqu
01-14-1996	11:31 pm	Pis
02-08-1996	09:31 pm	Ari
03-05-1996	09:01 pm	Tau
04-03-1996	10:26 am	Gem
08-07-1996	01:15 am	Can
09-07-1996	12:08 am	Leo
10-03-1996	10:22 pm	Vir
10-29-1996	07:03 am	Lib
11-22-1996	08:35 pm	Sco
12-17-1996	12:34 am	Sag
01-10-1997	12:32 am	Cap
02-02-1997	11:28 pm	Aqu
02-26-1997	11:02 pm	Pis
03-23-1997	12:27 am	Ari
04-16-1997	04:43 am	Tau
05-10-1997	12:21 pm	Gem

Date of Birth	Time of Birth	Venus Sign
06-03-1997	11:18 pm	Can
06-28-1997	01:38 pm	Leo
07-23-1997	08:17 am	Vir
08-17-1997	09:31 am	Lib
09-11-1997	09:17 pm	Sco
10-08-1997	03:26 am	Sag
11-05-1997	03:51 am	Cap
12-11-1997	11:40 pm	Aqu
04-06-1998	12:39 am	Pis
05-03-1998	02:17 pm	Ari
05-29-1998	06:33 pm	Tau
06-24-1998	07:28 am	Gem
07-19-1998	10:18 am	Can
08-13-1998	04:20 am	Leo
09-06-1998	02:25 pm	Vir
09-30-1998	06:14 pm	Lib
10-24-1998	06:07 pm	Sco
11-17-1998	04:07 pm	Sag
12-11-1998	01:34 pm	Cap
01-04-1999	11:26 am	Aqu
01-28-1999	11:17 am	Pis
02-21-1999	03:50 pm	Ari
03-18-1999	05:00 am	Tau
04-12-1999	08:18 am	Gem
05-08-1999	11:29 am	Can
06-05-1999	04:26 pm	Leo
07-12-1999	10:18 am	Vir

Date of Birth	Time of Birth	Venus Sign
11-08-1999	09:20 pm	Lib
12-05-1999	05:42 pm	Sco
12-30-1999	11:55 pm	Sag
01-24-2000	02:53 pm	Cap
02-17-2000	11:44 pm	Aqu
03-13-2000	06:37 am	Pis
04-06-2000	01:38 pm	Ari
04-30-2000	09:50 pm	Tau
05-25-2000	07:16 am	Gem
06-18-2000	05:16 pm	Can
07-13-2000	03:03 am	Leo
08-06-2000	12:33 pm	Vir
08-30-2000	10:36 pm	Lib
09-24-2000	10:26 am	Sco
10-19-2000	01:19 am	Sag
11-12-2000	09:15 pm	Cap
12-08-2000	03:49 am	Aqu
01-03-2001	01:14 pm	Pis
02-02-2001	02:15 pm	Ari
06-06-2001	05:26 am	Tau
07-05-2001	11:45 am	Gem
08-01-2001	07:19 am	Can
08-26-2001	11:13 pm	Leo
09-20-2001	09:10 pm	Vir
10-15-2001	06:43 am	Lib
11-08-2001	08:29 am	Sco
12-02-2001	06:12 am	Sag

Date of Birth	Time of Birth	Venus Sign
12-26-2001	02:26 am	Cap
01-18-2002	10:43 pm	Aqu
02-11-2002	08:18 pm	Pis
03-07-2002	08:42 pm	Ari
04-01-2002	01:40 am	Tau
04-25-2002	12:57 pm	Gem
05-20-2002	08:28 am	Can
06-14-2002	03:17 pm	Leo
07-10-2002	04:09 pm	Vir
08-07-2002	04:10 am	Lib
09-07-2002	10:05 pm	Sco
01-07-2003	08:08 am	Sag
02-04-2003	08:28 am	Cap
03-02-2003	07:41 am	Aqu
03-27-2003	01:15 pm	Pis
04-21-2003	11:19 am	Ari
05-16-2003	05:59 am	Tau
06-09-2003	10:33 pm	Gem
07-04-2003	12:39 pm	Can
07-28-2003	11:26 pm	Leo
08-22-2003	06:36 am	Vir
09-15-2003	10:59 am	Lib
10-09-2003	01:57 pm	Sco
11-02-2003	04:43 pm	Sag
11-26-2003	08:08 pm	Cap
12-21-2003	01:33 am	Aqu
01-14-2004	12:17 pm	Pis

Date of Birth	Time of Birth	Venus Sign
02-08-2004	11:21 am	Ari
03-05-2004	01:13 pm	Tau
04-03-2004	09:58 am	Gem
08-07-2004	06:03 am	Can
09-06-2004	05:16 pm	Leo
10-03-2004	12:21 pm	Vir
10-28-2004	07:40 pm	Lib
11-22-2004	08:32 am	Sco
12-16-2004	12:11 pm	Sag
01-09-2005	11:56 am	Cap
02-02-2005	10:43 am	Aqu
02-26-2005	10:08 am	Pis
03-22-2005	11:26 am	Ari
04-15-2005	03:38 pm	Tau
05-09-2005	11:15 pm	Gem
06-03-2005	10:18 am	Can
06-28-2005	12:54 am	Leo
07-22-2005	08:02 pm	Vir
08-16-2005	10:05 pm	Lib
09-11-2005	11:15 am	Sco
10-07-2005	08:01 pm	Sag
11-05-2005	03:11 am	Cap
12-15-2005	10:58 am	Aqu
04-05-2006	08:21 pm	Pis
05-03-2006	05:25 am	Ari
05-29-2006	07:42 am	Tau
06-23-2006	07:32 pm	Gem

Date of Birth	Time of Birth	Venus Sign
07-18-2006	09:42 pm	Can
08-12-2006	03:21 pm	Leo
09-06-2006	01:16 am	Vir
09-30-2006	05:03 am	Lib
10-24-2006	04:58 am	Sco
11-17-2006	03:03 am	Sag
12-11-2006	12:34 am	Cap
01-03-2007	10:32 pm	Aqu
01-27-2007	10:33 pm	Pis
02-21-2007	03:22 am	Ari
03-17-2007	05:01 pm	Tau
04-11-2007	09:16 pm	Gem
05-08-2007	02:29 am	Can
06-05-2007	01:00 pm	Leo
07-14-2007	01:24 pm	Vir
11-08-2007	04:06 pm	Lib
12-05-2007	08:30 am	Sco
12-30-2007	01:03 pm	Sag
01-24-2008	03:07 am	Cap
02-17-2008	11:23 am	Aqu
03-12-2008	05:52 pm	Pis
04-06-2008	12:36 am	Ari
04-30-2008	08:35 am	Tau
05-24-2008	05:53 pm	Gem
06-18-2008	03:49 am	Can
07-12-2008	01:40 pm	Leo
08-05-2008	11:20 pm	Vir

Date of Birth	Time of Birth	Venus Sign
08-30-2008	09:42 am	Lib
09-23-2008	10:00 pm	Sco
10-18-2008	01:31 pm	Sag
11-12-2008	10:25 am	Cap
12-07-2008	06:37 pm	Aqu
01-03-2009	07:36 am	Pis
02-02-2009	10:42 pm	Ari
06-06-2009	04:08 am	Tau
07-05-2009	03:23 am	Gem
07-31-2009	08:29 pm	Can
08-26-2009	11:12 am	Leo
09-20-2009	08:33 am	Vir
10-14-2009	05:47 pm	Lib
11-07-2009	07:24 pm	Sco
12-01-2009	05:04 pm	Sag
12-25-2009	01:18 pm	Cap
01-18-2010	09:35 am	Aqu
02-11-2010	07:11 am	Pis
03-07-2010	07:34 am	Ari
03-31-2010	2:36 pm	Tau
04-25-2010	12:06 am	Gem
05-19-2010	08:06 pm	Can
06-14-2010	03:51 am	Leo
07-10-2010	06:32 am	Vir
08-06-2010	10:48 pm	Lib
09-08-2010	10:45 am	Sco
01-07-2011	07:31 am	Sag

Date of Birth	Time of Birth	Venus Sign
02-04-2011	12:59 am	Cap
03-01-2011	09:40 pm	Aqu
03-27-2011	01:53 am	Pis
04-20-2011	11:07 pm	Ari
05-15-2011	05:13 pm	Tau
06-09-2011	09:24 am	Gem
07-03-2011	11:18 pm	Can
07-28-2011	09:59 am	Leo
08-21-2011	05:11 pm	Vir
09-14-2011	09:41 pm	Lib
10-09-2011	12:50 am	Sco
11-02-2011	03:52 am	Sag
11-26-2011	07:37 am	Cap
12-20-2011	01:27 pm	Aqu
01-14-2012	12:48 am	Pis
02-08-2012	01:02 am	Ari
03-05-2012	05:25 am	Tau
04-03-2012	10:19 am	Gem
08-07-2012	08:44 am	Can
09-06-2012	09:49 am	Leo
10-03-2012	02:00 am	Vir
10-28-2012	08:05 am	Lib
11-21-2012	08:21 pm	Sco
12-15-2012	11:39 pm	Sag
01-08-2013	11:12 pm	Cap
02-01-2013	09:47 pm	Aqu
02-25-2013	09:04 pm	Pis

Date of Birth	Time of Birth	Venus Sign
03-21-2013	10:16 pm	Ari
04-15-2013	02:26 am	Tau
05-09-2013	10:04 am	Gem
06-02-2013	09:13 pm	Can
06-27-2013	12:04 pm	Leo
07-22-2013	07:42 am	Vir
08-16-2013	10:37 am	Lib
09-11-2013	01:16 am	Sco
10-07-2013	12:55 pm	Sag
11-05-2013	03:43 am	Cap
03-05-2014	04:04 pm	Aqu
04-05-2014	03:32 pm	Pis
05-02-2014	08:22 pm	Ari
05-28-2014	08:46 pm	Tau
06-23-2014	07:34 am	Gem
07-18-2014	09:07 am	Can
08-12-2014	02:24 am	Leo
09-05-2014	12:08 pm	Vir
09-29-2014	03:53 pm	Lib
10-23-2014	03:53 pm	Sco
11-16-2014	02:04 pm	Sag
12-10-2014	11:43 am	Cap
01-03-2015	09:49 am	Aqu
01-27-2015	10:00 am	Pis
02-20-2015	03:06 pm	Ari
03-17-2015	05:15 am	Tau
04-11-2015	10:29 am	Gem

Date of Birth	Time of Birth	Venus Sign
05-07-2015	05:53 pm	Can
06-05-2015	10:34 am	Leo
07-18-2015	05:39 pm	Vir
11-08-2015	10:32 am	Lib
12-04-2015	11:16 pm	Sco
12-30-2015	02:17 am	Sag

Index

About the Author

PHYLLIS VEGA is a practicing astrologer and tarot reader, and has been a New Age counselor for more than three decades. She is the author of numerous books, including: *Lovestrology*; *What Your Birthday Reveals About You*; *Sydney Omarr's Sun, Moon, and You*; *Sydney Omarr's Astrology, Love, Sex, and You*; *Celtic Astrology*, *Power Tarot*, coauthored with Trish MacGregor; and *Romancing the Tarot.* Ms. Vega resides in Miami, Florida, and can be contacted through her website: *www.geocities.com/phyllisvega*.

Printed in the United States
By Bookmasters